■ SCHOLASTIC

BOOK OF WORLD RECORDS 2006

By Jenifer Corr Morse

A GEORGIAN BAY BOOK

SCHOLASTIC ⚲ REFERENCE

To Isabelle Nicole—May you always find wonder in the world.
–JCM

CREATED AND PRODUCED BY GEORGIAN BAY ASSOCIATES, LLC

Georgian Bay Staff
Bruce S. Glassman, Executive Editor
Jenifer Corr Morse, Photo Editor
Calico Harington, Design

Scholastic Reference Staff
Kenneth R. Wright, Editorial Director
Mary Varilla Jones, Editor
Brenda Murray, Assistant Editor
Nancy Sabato, Art Director
Tatiana Sperhacke, Designer
Dwayne Howard, Photo Researcher

In most cases, the graphs in this book represent the top five record holders in each category.
However, in some graphs, we have chosen to list well-known or common people, places,
animals, or things that will help you better understand how extraordinary the record holder
is. These may not be the top five in the category. Additionally, some graphs have fewer than
five entries because so few people or objects reflect the necessary criteria.

ISBN 0-439-75518-2

10 9 8 7 6 5 4 3   06 07 08 09
Printed in the U.S.A.   23
First printing, October 2005

Contents

Nature Records   130

U.S. Records   205

Human-Made Records   256

Money and Business Records   278

Popular Culture Records

Music • Television • Movies • Theater • Art

World's Top-Earning Male Singer

Prince

Prince—the artist that was formerly known as a symbol—earned $90 million in 2004. The artist's highly successful *Musicology* tour was the source for most of his income. The concerts were performed in 69 cities and drew about 1.5 million people—more than any other tour that year. Prince performed many of his classic hits, including "Little Red Corvette," "1999," "Purple Rain," "When Doves Cry," and "Let's Go Crazy." In March, the singer was inducted into the Rock and Roll Hall of Fame. During his 25-year career, Prince has sold more than 100 million records.

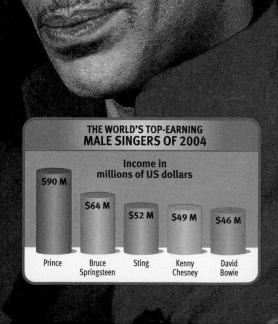

THE WORLD'S TOP-EARNING MALE SINGERS OF 2004

Income in millions of US dollars

Prince	Bruce Springsteen	Sting	Kenny Chesney	David Bowie
$90 M	$64 M	$52 M	$49 M	$46 M

World's Top-Earning Female Singer

Madonna

Madonna made a record-breaking $125 million in 2004. Much of the Material Girl's success came from her blockbuster Reinvention Tour. She sold out all but one of her 56 performances worldwide, and averaged a profit of about $2 million a night. In addition to singing some of her most popular hits—which span more than two decades—Madonna also included tracks from her latest CD, *American Life*. The singer and actress has also recently added children's book author to her bio. Her first book, *The English Roses*, has sold more than half a million copies since it was published in September 2003.

THE WORLD'S TOP-EARNING FEMALE SINGERS OF 2004

Income in millions of US dollars

Singer	Income
Madonna	$125 M
Celine Dion	$77 M
Shania Twain	$63 M
Bette Midler	$53 M
Britney Spears	$31 M

World's Best-Selling Single of All Time

Candle in the Wind 1997

BEST-SELLING SINGLES OF ALL TIME

Sales in millions

37.5 M	31.2 M	26.0 M	12.4 M	10.6 M
"Candle in the Wind 1997," Elton John	"White Christmas," Bing Crosby	"Rock Around the Clock," Bill Haley and the Comets	"I Want to Hold Your Hand," The Beatles	"Hey Jude," The Beatles

ELTON JOHN
Something About The Way You Look Tonight
Candle In The Wind 1997
In loving memory of Diana, Princess of Wales

CD 2 TITLES

Elton John's single "Candle in the Wind 1997" sold a record-shattering 37.5 million copies since its release that year. John had first released the song in 1973 to honor the memory of Marilyn Monroe. When John's close friend Princess Diana was killed in a tragic car crash in 1997, John rewrote the song as a tribute to her and performed it at her funeral. John felt that this song was also especially appropriate for the princess because both women were constantly hounded by the press. John also earned a Grammy® Award for "Candle in the Wind 1997" for Best Male Pop Vocal Performance later that year.

World's Best-Selling Album

Thriller

To date, Michael Jackson's smash hit *Thriller* has sold approximately 52 million copies. It was first released on March 16, 1982, and quickly became one of the most popular albums of all time—both nationally and internationally. *Thriller* was released on the Epic record label and was produced by mastermind Quincy Jones. The album featured many pop singles, including "Beat It," "Billie Jean," and "Wanna Be Startin' Somethin'." *Thriller* received eight Grammy® Awards and contained six top-10 singles.

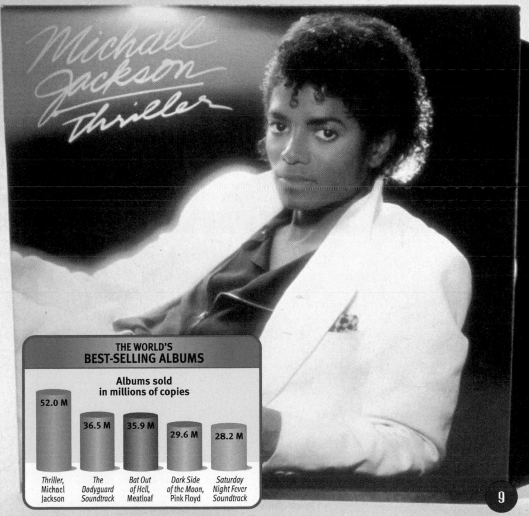

THE WORLD'S BEST-SELLING ALBUMS

Albums sold in millions of copies

Thriller, Michael Jackson	The Bodyguard Soundtrack	Bat Out of Hell, Meatloaf	Dark Side of the Moon, Pink Floyd	Saturday Night Fever Soundtrack
52.0 M	36.5 M	35.9 M	29.6 M	28.2 M

United States' Best-Selling

Recording Group

The Beatles

Since their first official recording session in September 1962, the Beatles have sold more than 168 million copies of their music. In the two years that followed, they had 26 top-40 singles. The "Fab Four," as they were called, were John Lennon, Paul McCartney, George Harrison, and Ringo Starr. Together they recorded many albums that are now considered rock masterpieces, such as *Rubber Soul*, *Sgt. Pepper's Lonely Hearts Club Band*, and *The White Album*. The group broke up in 1969. In 2001, however, their newly released greatest hits album—*The Beatles 1*—reached the top of the charts. In January 2003, some 500 never-before-heard tapes of the Beatles' recording sessions were discovered to the delight of fans around the world.

THE UNITED STATES' BEST-SELLING RECORDING GROUPS

Millions of copies sold

The Beatles	Led Zeppelin	The Eagles	Pink Floyd	AC/DC
168.5 M	107.5 M	89.0 M	73.5 M	66.0 M

World's
Top-Earning Band

The Rolling Stones

THE WORLD'S TOP-EARNING BANDS OF 2004

Earnings in millions of US dollars

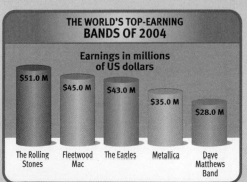

The Rolling Stones	Fleetwood Mac	The Eagles	Metallica	Dave Matthews Band
$51.0 M	$45.0 M	$43.0 M	$35.0 M	$28.0 M

Rock legends The Rolling Stones brought in $51 million in 2004. After celebrating their 40th anniversary in 2002, the Stones continued with the second part of their two-year *Forty Licks* concert tour. Some songs that are performed at each show include "Start Me Up," "Brown Sugar," "Jumpin' Jack Flash," and "(I Can't Get No) Satisfaction." Band members Mick Jagger, Keith Richards, Ron Wood, and Charlie Watts also released the best-selling DVD collection *Four Flicks*, which features footage of several concerts from the tour.

United States' Best-Selling Male
Recording Artist

Elvis Presley has sold more than 116.5 million records since he first signed with RCA Records back in 1955. Presley's unique sound and dance moves captured fans' attention around the world. Known as the King of Rock and Roll, Presley also holds the record for the solo singer with the most chart hits at 151. Some of his most famous songs include *Love Me Tender*, *Blue Suede Shoes*, *Jailhouse Rock*, and *All Shook Up*. Presley also had an impressive film career. He appeared in more than 30 films, which earned a combined total of about $150 million at the box office. Presley died in 1977.

Elvis Presley

THE UNITED STATES' BEST-SELLING
MALE RECORDING ARTISTS

Units sold, in millions

Elvis Presley	Garth Brooks	Billy Joel	Elton John	Bruce Springsteen
116.5 M	105.0 M	78.5 M	69.0 M	61.5 M

United States' Best-Selling Female
Recording Artist

Barbra Streisand

During her 39 years as a singer, Barbra Streisand has sold over 70 million copies of her work. She has recorded more than 50 albums and has more gold albums than any other entertainer in history. Streisand has 47 gold albums, 28 platinum albums, 13 multiplatinum albums, 8 gold singles, 5 platinum singles, and 5 gold videos. Some of her recordings include *People*, *Color Me Barbra*, *Emotion*, and *Higher Ground*. Some of her best-known film work includes roles in *Funny Girl*, *The Way We Were*, *Yentl*, and *The Prince of Tides*. Streisand has won 10 Grammys®, 2 Academy Awards®, 6 Emmy® Awards, and 11 Golden Globes.

THE UNITED STATES' BEST-SELLING FEMALE RECORDING ARTISTS

Units sold, in millions

Barbra Streisand	Madonna	Mariah Carey	Whitney Houston	Celine Dion
70.5 M	60.0 M	57.5 M	54.0 M	47.0 M

13

Singer with the Most
Country Music Awards

Vince Gill

Country superstar Vince Gill has racked up 18 Country Music Awards. Since his debut album *Turn Me Loose* in 1984, Gill has been a fan favorite. He won his first Country Music Award in 1990 for Single of the Year with "When I Call Your Name." Since then, he has won Male Vocalist of the Year five times, Song of the Year four times, Vocal Event of the Year four times, Entertainer of the Year twice, and Album of the Year twice. Several of Gill's albums have gone gold and platinum, and he was asked to join the Grand Ole Opry in 1992.

SINGERS WITH THE MOST
COUNTRY MUSIC AWARDS

Number of awards

18	16	14	11	10
Vince Gill	Alan Jackson	Brooks & Dunn	Garth Brooks	Dixie Chicks

Most Popular
Television Show

CSI

MOST POPULAR TELEVISION SHOWS
Average Nielsen rating

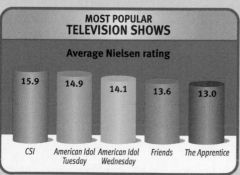

CSI	American Idol Tuesday	American Idol Wednesday	Friends	The Apprentice
15.9	14.9	14.1	13.6	13.0

CSI is a smash hit for CBS, averaging 15.9 million viewers each Thursday. The hour-long drama features a team of forensic specialists who work for the Las Vegas Police Department's Crime Scene Investigation unit. Gil Grissom, played by William Petersen, leads the team of scientists, including Sara (Jorja Fox), Catherine (Marg Helgenberger), Warrick (Gary Dourdan), and Nick (George Eads). The show has been so popular, it has inspired two spin-offs—*CSI: Miami* and *CSI: New York*.

Highest-Paid
TV Actress

Debra
Messing

Debra Messing earns an impressive $400,000 an episode for her role as Grace Adler on the popular NBC sitcom *Will & Grace*. Averaging 23 episodes each year, Messing's annual TV salary totals more than $9 million. Since she began her role as the ditzy interior designer in 1998, Messing has won an Emmy® Award, five Golden Globe Awards, and a TV Guide Award. *Will & Grace* has won 12 Emmy® Awards and has been the second-highest rated comedy for the last four years.

HIGHEST-PAID
TV ACTRESSES

Money earned per episode during the 2004–2005 season, in US dollars

$400,000

$144,000

$120,000

$100,000

$70,000

| Debra Messing, Will & Grace | Marg Helgenberger, CSI | Jorja Fox, CSI | Jane Kaczmarek, Malcolm in the Middle | Allison Janney, The West Wing |

Highest-Paid
TV Actor

James Gandolfini

James Gandolfini takes home $1 million for each episode of HBO's monster hit *The Sopranos*. Gandolfini plays Tony Soprano, the head of a New Jersey mobster family in the popular crime drama. Since *The Sopranos* began in 1999, Gandolfini has won an Emmy® Award, four SAG Awards, and three Golden Globe Awards. On the big screen, Gandolfini is also a big hit. Some of his movie credits include *Get Shorty* (1995), *Crimson Tide* (1995), *The Mexican* (2001), and *Surviving Christmas* (2004).

**HIGHEST-PAID
TV ACTORS**

Money earned per episode during
the 2004–2005 season, in US dollars

$1.0 M — James Gandolfini, *The Sopranos*
$500,000 — Matt LeBlanc, *Joey*
$400,000 — Eric McCormack, *Will & Grace*
$350,000 — William Petersen, *CSI*
$300,000 — Martin Sheen, *The West Wing*

17

Most Emmy® Awards In a Single Season

The West Wing

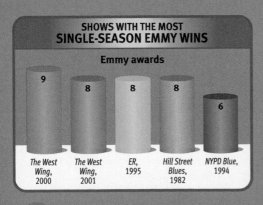

SHOWS WITH THE MOST SINGLE-SEASON EMMY WINS

Emmy awards

Show	Awards
The West Wing, 2000	9
The West Wing, 2001	8
ER, 1995	8
Hill Street Blues, 1982	8
NYPD Blue, 1994	6

The West Wing—an NBC drama about life in the White House—won a record-setting nine awards at the 52nd Primetime Emmy® Awards in September 2000. Some of the awards won that night included Outstanding Drama Series, Best Supporting Actor, and Best Supporting Actress. The cast of *The West Wing* includes many distinguished actors, including Martin Sheen as President Josiah Bartlet, John Spencer as Chief of Staff Leo McGarry, Bradley Whitford as Deputy Chief of Staff Josh Lyman, and Stockard Channing as First Lady Abby Bartlet. Allison Janney, who plays Press Secretary C.J. Cregg, earned two Emmy® Awards in 2000 and 2001. *The West Wing* has also won a Peabody Award, a Golden Globe, and several Television Critics Association Awards.

Actor with the Highest Career
Box-Office Earnings

Samuel L. Jackson

During his impressive career, Samuel L. Jackson has appeared in more than 80 movies, and leads all other actors with box-office earnings, totaling more than $3.3 billion! Some of his most well-known movies include *Do The Right Thing* (1989), *Jurassic Park* (1993), *Pulp Fiction* (1994), *Die Hard with a Vengeance* (1995), and *Coach Carter* (2005). Most recently he appears in *Star Wars: Episode III— Revenge of the Sith* as Mace Windu. Jackson was honored with a star on the Hollywood Walk of Fame in 2000.

**ACTORS WITH THE HIGHEST
CAREER BOX-OFFICE EARNINGS**

Earnings in billions
of US dollars

Samuel L. Jackson	Harrison Ford	Tom Hanks	Eddie Murphy	Tom Cruise
$3.31 B	$3.26 B	$3.08 B	$2.91 B	$2.67 B

World's Highest Paid
Actress

Julia Roberts

American superstar Julia Roberts was paid a record-breaking $25 million to portray art professor Katherine Watson in *Mona Lisa Smile*. Roberts made her professional film debut in 1988 in the movie *Mystic Pizza*. She won an Academy Award® for Best Actress for her work in *Erin Brockovich* in 2000. She has also received Oscar® nominations for her roles in *Steel Magnolias* and *Pretty Woman*. Some of Roberts's other well-known movies include *Ocean's Eleven*, *Runaway Bride*, and *America's Sweethearts*.

THE WORLD'S HIGHEST-PAID ACTRESSES

Approximate salary per movie, in millions of US dollars

$25.0 M	$20.0 M	$20.0 M	$20.0 M	$17.5 M
Julia Roberts, *Mona Lisa Smile*, 2003	Cameron Diaz, *Charlie's Angels: Full Throttle*, 2003	Julia Roberts, *The Mexican*, 2001	Julia Roberts, *Erin Brockovich*, 2000	Cameron Diaz, *Gangs of New York*, 2002

World's Highest-Paid Actor

Arnold Schwarzenegger earned a record-shattering $30 million for his role as T-850 in *Terminator 3: Rise of the Machines* in 2003. In the third installment of the sci-fi action movie saga that began in 1984, he reprises his role as the Terminator. Schwarzenegger's first title role in a movie was *Conan the Barbarian* in 1982 for which he earned $250,000. In 1996, Schwarzenegger earned $20 million for *Jingle All the Way*. By the late 1990s, his salary had increased to $25 million for movies such as *Batman & Robin* (1997), *End of Days* (1999), and *The 6th Day* (2000). In 2003, Schwarzenegger expanded his career to include politics when he was elected as the governor of California.

THE WORLD'S HIGHEST-PAID ACTORS

Salary in millions of US dollars

$30 M	$25 M	$25 M	$25 M	$25 M
Arnold Schwarzenegger, *Terminator 3*, 2003	Tom Cruise, *The Last Samurai*, 2003	Mel Gibson, *Signs*, 2002	Chris Tucker, *Rush Hour 2*, 2001	Jim Carrey, *Bruce Almighty*, 2003

Arnold Schwarzenegger

Actor with the Most
MTV Movie Awards

Jim Carrey

Jim Carrey has picked up nine MTV Movie Awards since the network began the ceremony in 1992. He has won four awards for Best Comedic Performance (*Dumb and Dumber*—1994; *Ace Ventura: When Nature Calls*—1995; *The Cable Guy*—1996; *Liar Liar*—1997). He picked up one award for Best Kiss (*Dumb and Dumber*). Carrey won Best Male Performance for *Ace Ventura: When Nature Calls* and *The Truman Show* (1998). He also earned two awards for Best Villain in *The Cable Guy* and *How the Grinch Stole Christmas* (2000).

ACTORS WITH THE
MOST MTV MOVIE AWARDS

Number of awards

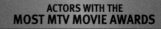

Jim Carrey	Mike Myers	Adam Sandler	Keanu Reeves	Will Smith
9	5	5	4	4

Actress with the Most
MTV Movie Awards

Alicia Silverstone

ACTRESSES WITH THE MOST MTV MOVIE AWARDS

Number of awards

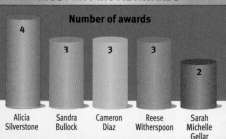

Alicia Silverstone	Sandra Bullock	Cameron Diaz	Reese Witherspoon	Sarah Michelle Gellar
4	3	3	3	2

Alicia Silverstone has won four MTV Movie Awards—more than any other actress. She earned two awards—Best Villain and Best Breakthrough Performance—for her work on the 1993 movie *The Crush* when she was just 15 years old. Her next two awards—Most Desirable Female and Best Female Performance—came for the popular 1995 comedy *Clueless*. MTV viewers also know Silverstone from her appearances in several Aerosmith videos. The MTV Movie Awards are based on viewers' votes. The Awards are known for their offbeat award categories, such as Best On-Screen Kiss and Best Action Sequence.

23

World's Largest Pre-Approved Movie Budget

Terminator 3

THE WORLD'S LARGEST PRE-APPROVED MOVIE BUDGETS

Pre-approved budget in millions of US dollars

$170 M	$140 M	$140 M	$135 M	$135 M
Terminator 3, 2003	Armageddon, 1998	The Last Samurai, 2003	Master and Commander, 2003	Pearl Harbor, 2001

Terminator 3: Rise of the Machines had an approved budget of $170 million. Although other movies had budgets that ultimately grew much higher during production, this is the first movie to get the go-ahead for such a large budget before the movie even started filming. *Terminator 3* opened in July 2003 starring Arnold Schwarzenegger as the Terminator, Nick Stahl as John Connor, and Kristanna Loken as T-X. In the movie, the Terminator returns to save Connor from T-X, a sophisticated cyborg-killing machine. The original *Terminator* was released in 1984, and the sequel, *Terminator 2: Judgment Day*, came out in 1991.

Most Successful Movie
Opening Weekend

MOVIES WITH THE
BEST OPENING WEEKENDS

Weekend earnings in millions of US dollars

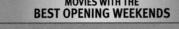

$114.8 M	$108.0 M	$92.6 M	$91.8 M	$90.3 M
Spider-Man 5/3/02	Shrek 2 5/19/04	Harry Potter and the Prisoner of Azkaban 6/04/04	The Matrix Reloaded 5/15/03	Harry Potter and the Sorcerer's Stone 11/16/01

On the first weekend in May 2002, the comic book thriller *Spider-Man* earned an amazing $114.8 million. The box-office receipts from this one weekend made up more than a quarter of the film's total gross of $404 million. The Sony film—which opened in more than 3,600 movie theaters across the country—starred Tobey Maguire as Spider-Man and Kirsten Dunst as his love interest, Mary Jane Watson. Willem Dafoe played the movie's villain—the Green Goblin.

World's Top-Grossing Kids' Movie

Snow White and the Seven Dwarfs

In the 68 years since its debut, Walt Disney's *Snow White and the Seven Dwarfs* has earned an amazing $1.03 billion in box-office receipts to date. (To compare the success of films throughout the decades, it is necessary to adjust for inflation.) More than 750 artists were used during the three-year production. *Snow White and the Seven Dwarfs* was the first-ever animated feature film, and it cost $1.4 million to make. Many of the songs in the movie, including "Some Day My Prince Will Come" and "Whistle While You Work," have become true American classics.

THE WORLD'S TOP-GROSSING KIDS' MOVIES

Box-office receipts in billions and millions of constant dollars

$1.03 B	$977 M	$912 M	$877 M	$865 M
Snow White and the Seven Dwarfs, 1937	Harry Potter and the Sorcerer's Stone, 2001	Shrek 2, 2004	Harry Potter and the Chamber of Secrets, 2002	Finding Nemo, 2003

World's Top-Grossing
Movie

Titanic

The blockbuster movie *Titanic* has grossed more than $600 million in the United States and more than $1.8 billion worldwide. Directed by James Cameron in 1997, this action-packed drama/romance is set aboard the White Star Line's lavish *RMS Titanic* in 1912. The two main characters, wealthy Rose DeWitt Bukater and the poor immigrant Jack Dawson—played by Kate Winslet and Leonardo DiCaprio—meet, fall in love, and are separated as the *Titanic* sinks into the North Atlantic on the morning of April 15, 1912.

THE WORLD'S TOP-GROSSING MOVIES

Gross income in billions and millions of US dollars

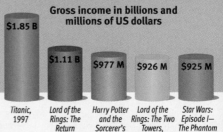

$1.85 B	$1.11 B	$977 M	$926 M	$925 M
Titanic, 1997	Lord of the Rings: The Return of the King, 2003	Harry Potter and the Sorcerer's Stone, 2001	Lord of the Rings: The Two Towers, 2002	Star Wars: Episode I— The Phantom Menace, 1999

Movies with the Most Oscars®

Ben-Hur, The Lord of the Rings: The Return of the King, Titanic

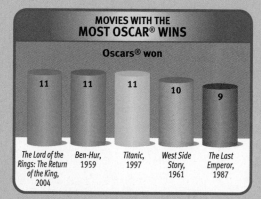

MOVIES WITH THE MOST OSCAR® WINS

Oscars® won

The Lord of the Rings: The Return of the King, 2004	Ben-Hur, 1959	Titanic, 1997	West Side Story, 1961	The Last Emperor, 1987
11	11	11	10	9

Cast and crew members with some of the 11 Oscars® for *The Lord of the Rings: The Return of the King*

The only three films in Hollywood history to win 11 Academy Awards are *Ben-Hur*, *The Lord of the Rings: The Return of the King*, and *Titanic*. Some of the Oscar wins for *Ben-Hur*—a biblical epic based on an 1880 novel by General Lew Wallace—include Best Picture and Best Score. *The Lord of the Rings: The Return of the King* is the final film in the epic trilogy based on the works of J.R.R. Tolkien. With 11 awards, it is the most successful movie in Academy Awards history because it won in every category in which it was nominated. Some of these wins include Best Picture, Best Director (Peter Jackson), and Best Costume. Some of *Titanic's* Oscars include Best Picture and Best Director (James Cameron).

Country That Makes the
Most Movies

India

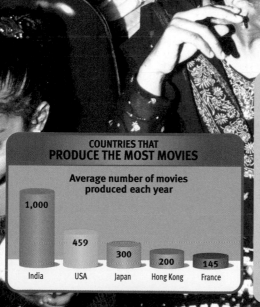

COUNTRIES THAT
PRODUCE THE MOST MOVIES

Average number of movies produced each year

India	1,000
USA	459
Japan	300
Hong Kong	200
France	145

Filmmakers in India produce an average of 1,000 movies annually. With that availability, it's not surprising that movies have replaced theater as the favorite national pastime of India. Bombay (Mumbai) has earned the nickname "Bollywood," for its Hollywood-like productions. Bollywood movies generally average three hours in length and usually include several song-and-dance scenes. Their budgets are much lower than American-made movies, however, with most averaging below $6 million. Many Indian movies also enjoy a worldwide audience. *Monsoon Wedding* received a Golden Globe nomination in 2001.

29

World's Longest-Running Broadway Show

Cats

Since its debut, the cast of the Broadway hit *Cats* performed 7,485 shows. That means they averaged one show each day for almost 19 years! The show began at the New London Theatre in England in May 1981 and later opened at the Winter Garden on Broadway in October 1982. This tale about the "jellicle cats" had 2,500 props built into its set and used more than 100 props on stage. There were about 250 different costumes and more than 35 wigs made from yak hair. The show has been seen by more than 50 million people worldwide and has grossed more than $2 billion. *Cats* closed in September 2000.

**THE WORLD'S
LONGEST-RUNNING BROADWAY SHOWS**

Total performances*

7,485	7,215	6,680	6,137	5,959
Cats, 1982–2000	The Phantom of the Opera, 1988–	Les Misérables, 1987–2003	A Chorus Line, 1975–1990	Oh! Calcutta!, 1969–1972

*As of May 15, 2005

Play with the
Most Tony Awards

The Producers

The Producers took home twelve of its record-breaking fifteen Tony nominations in March 2001. The Broadway smash took home awards for Best Musical, Best Original Score, Best Book, Best Direction of a Musical, Best Choreography, Best Orchestration, Best Scenic Design, Best Costume Design, Best Lighting Design, Best Actor in a Musical, Best Featured Actor in a Musical, and Best Actress in a Musical. *The Producers*, which starred Nathan Lane and Matthew Broderick, is a stage adaptation of Mel Brooks' 1968 movie. He wrote the lyrics and music for sixteen new songs for the stage version.

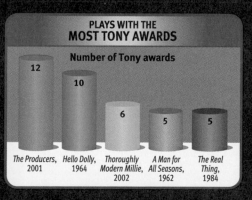

**PLAYS WITH THE
MOST TONY AWARDS**

Number of Tony awards

The Producers, 2001	Hello Dolly, 1964	Thoroughly Modern Millie, 2002	A Man for All Seasons, 1962	The Real Thing, 1984
12	10	6	5	5

Most Valuable Auctioned
Painting

Boy with a Pipe

Boy with a Pipe, an oil painting created by Spanish artist Pablo Picasso in 1905, sold for $93 million at a Sotheby's auction in 2004. When the auctioneer's commission is included, the anonymous bidder paid a grand total of $104.1 million. The painting was completed during Picasso's "rose period," a time between 1904 and 1906 when the artist used the color in many of his creations. *Boy with a Pipe* is one of the few Picasso paintings that is not in a museum. The painting was sold as part of a fundraiser for the Greentree Foundation, which promotes international peace. The previous owners, John and Betsey Whitney, paid about $30,000 for it in 1950.

THE WORLD'S MOST VALUABLE PAINTINGS SOLD AT AUCTION

Price in millions of US dollars

$93.0 M	$82.5 M	$76.7 M	$71.0 M	$65.0 M
Boy with a Pipe, Picasso	Portrait of Dr. Gachet, van Gogh	The Massacre of the Innocents, Peter Paul Rubens	Au Moulin de la Galette, Pierre-Auguste Renoir	Portrait de l'Artiste Sans Barbe, van Gogh

World's Most Expensive Painting By a Woman Artist

The Conversation

THE WORLD'S MOST EXPENSIVE WOMEN'S PAINTINGS SOLD AT AUCTION

Price paid in millions of US dollars

$4.1 M	$4.0 M	$3.7 M	$3.5 M	$3.5 M
The Conversation, Mary Cassatt	Cache-cache, Berthe Morisot	In the Box, Mary Cassatt	Cache-cache, Berthe Morisot	Mother, Sara and the Baby, Mary Cassatt

On May 11, 1988, Mary Cassatt's oil painting *The Conversation* sold for $4.1 million at a Christie's auction and is now part of a private collection. Similar to *The Conversation*, the majority of Cassatt's paintings and pastel sketches feature women and children participating in everyday activities. Cassatt studied at the Pennsylvania Academy of Fine Arts before studying art in Europe in 1865. After settling in Paris, she began to work with acclaimed Impressionists Edouard Manet and Edgar Degas. Cassatt was greatly influenced by both their subjects and their techniques.

Science and Technology Records

Vehicles • Technology • Computers
Video Games • Space • Solar System

World's Fastest Production Motorcycle

Suzuki GSX1300R Hayabusa

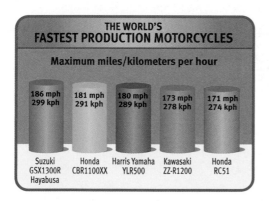

THE WORLD'S FASTEST PRODUCTION MOTORCYCLES

Maximum miles/kilometers per hour

Suzuki GSX1300R Hayabusa	Honda CBR1100XX	Harris Yamaha YLR500	Kawasaki ZZ-R1200	Honda RC51
186 mph 299 kph	181 mph 291 kph	180 mph 289 kph	173 mph 278 kph	171 mph 274 kph

This sleek speed machine, which is named after one of the world's fastest birds, is able to reach a maximum speed of 186 miles (299 km) per hour. That's about three times faster than the speed limit on most major highways. In 1999, the Hayabusa won several major awards, including Motorcycle of the Year and Best Superbike. Its aerodynamic shape, four-cylinder engine, and six-speed transmission make the bike very popular with motorcycle enthusiasts. In 2001, motorcycle manufacturers set a guideline stating that no new production motorcycles will have a top speed above 186 miles (299 km) per hour for safety reasons.

World's Fastest
Production Car

Bugatti Veyron

THE WORLD'S FASTEST PRODUCTION CARS

Maximum miles/kilometers per hour

Bugatti Veyron	Koenigsegg CCR	Koenigsegg CC85	McLaren F1	Ferrari Enzo
248 mph 400 kph	245 mph 395 kph	242 mph 390 kph	240 mph 386 kph	217 mph 349 kph

The Volkswagen Bugatti Veyron can cruise along at a top speed of 248 miles (400 km) per hour. In fact, it can reach 62 miles (100 km) per hour in just 2 seconds, and accelerate to 186 miles (300 km) per hour in only 14 seconds. The seven-speed semi-manual transmission takes less than a quarter of a second to change gears. The Bugatti Veyron is powered by an 8.0-liter W-16 engine and is made of super-lightweight aluminum and magnesium. This ultimate sports car sells for about $1.3 million, and only 300 of them will be produced. Buyers can also opt to jazz up their new Veyron by adding two one-carat diamonds to the speedometer.

EB 18/4 "Veyron"

World's Largest Yacht

Abdul Aziz

THE WORLD'S LARGEST YACHTS

Length in feet/meters

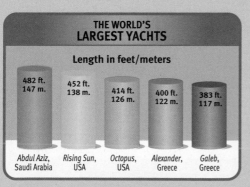

482 ft. 147 m.	452 ft. 138 m.	414 ft. 126 m.	400 ft. 122 m.	383 ft. 117 m.
Abdul Aziz, Saudi Arabia	Rising Sun, USA	Octopus, USA	Alexander, Greece	Galeb, Greece

The largest yacht in the world measures an astounding 482 feet (147 m) long—about half the length of a commercial ocean liner! It features 60 guest rooms, two swimming pools, and a helicopter pad. It was built in the Vospers Ship Yard in England in 1984. This royal yacht was named after its owner, Prince Abdul Aziz of Saudi Arabia. When he acquired the yacht in 1987, it was estimated to be worth more than $100 million in U.S. currency. At the time, the prince was just 18 years old, but was already worth about $1 billion.

World's Fastest Land Vehicle

Thrust SSC

The Thrust SSC, which stands for SuperSonic Car, reached a speed of 763 miles (1,228 km) per hour on October 15, 1997. At that speed, a car could make it from San Francisco to New York City in less than 4 hours. The Thrust SSC is propelled by two jet engines capable of 110,000 horsepower. The Thrust SSC runs on jet fuel, using about 5 gallons (19 l) per second. It only takes approximately five seconds for this supersonic car to reach its top speed. It is 54 feet (16.5 m) long and weighs 7 tons (6.4 t).

VEHICLES WITH THE FASTEST SPEEDS ON LAND

Speed in miles/kilometers per hour

763 mph 1,228 kph	633 mph 1,019 kph	622 mph 1,001 kph	600 mph 966 kph	576 mph 927 kph
Thrust SSC, 1997	Thrust 2, 1983	Blue Flame, 1970	Spirit of America, 1965	Green Monster, 1965

World's Largest
Cruise Ship

Queen Mary 2

The *Queen Mary 2* measures 1,132 feet (345 m) long, some 236 feet (72 m) high, and weighs 151,400 gross tons (137,320 t). This gigantic luxury ship is longer than three football fields, but can still move at a top speed of 35 miles (56 km) per hour. The $800 million ship can accommodate 2,620 passengers and 1,253 crew members. On board, guests can enjoy such amenities as the Canyon Ranch Spa, a planetarium, virtual reality golf, a disco, and the largest ballroom at sea. The *Queen Mary 2* made her maiden voyage from Southampton, England, to Fort Lauderdale, Florida, in 2004. First class passengers paid up to $38,000 for the historic trip.

THE WORLD'S LARGEST CRUISE SHIPS

Length

Queen Mary 2	Voyager of the Seas	Adventure of the Seas	Explorer of the Seas	Navigator of the Seas
1,132 ft. 345 m	1,020 ft. 311 m	1,020 ft. 311 m	1,020 ft. 311 m	1,020 ft. 311 m

World's Fastest Plane

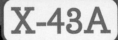

X-43A

THE WORLD'S FASTEST PLANES

Speed in miles/kilometers per hour

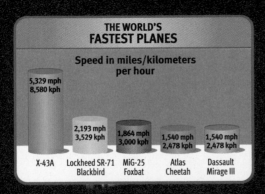

X-43A	Lockheed SR-71 Blackbird	MiG-25 Foxbat	Atlas Cheetah	Dassault Mirage III
5,329 mph 8,580 kph	2,193 mph 3,529 kph	1,864 mph 3,000 kph	1,540 mph 2,478 kph	1,540 mph 2,478 kph

NASA's experimental X-43A plane reached a top speed of Mach 7—or seven times the speed of sound—on a test flight over the Pacific Ocean in March 2004. The X-43A was mounted on top of a Pegasus rocket booster and was carried into the sky by a B-52 aircraft. The booster was then fired, taking the X-43A about 95,000 feet (28,956 m) above the ground. The rocket was detached from the unmanned X-43A, and the plane flew unassisted for several minutes. At this rate of 5,329 miles (8,580 km) per hour, a plane could fly from Los Angeles to New York City in just 32 minutes.

World's Fastest
Roller Coaster

Kingda Ka

THE WORLD'S FASTEST
ROLLER COASTERS

Speed
(miles per hour/kilometers per hour)

Kingda Ka, USA	Top Thrill Dragster, USA	Dodonpa, Japan	Superman the Escape, USA	Tower of Terror, Australia
128 mph 206 kph	120 mph 193 kph	106 mph 172 kph	100 mph 161 kph	100 mph 161 kph

Kingda Ka—the newest coaster at Six Flags Great Adventure in Jackson, New Jersey—can launch riders straight up a track at a top speed of 128 miles (206 km) per hour. This hydraulic launch coaster reaches its top speed in less than 4 seconds. Kingda Ka is also the world's tallest rollercoaster at 456 feet (139 m). In addition to the horizontal rocket that starts the ride, the coaster also features a few breathtaking drops and spiral turns. The 50-second ride is located in the Golden Kingdom section of the park.

World's Biggest
Monster Truck

The Bigfoot 5 truly is a monster—it measures 15.4 feet (4.7 m) high! That's about three times the height of an average car. Bigfoot 5 has 10-foot- (3-m) high Firestone Tundra tires each weighing 2,400 pounds (1,088 kg), giving the truck a total weight of about 38,000 pounds (17,236 kg). This modified 1996 Ford F250 pickup truck is owned by Bob Chandler of St. Louis, Missouri. The great weight of this monster truck makes it too large to race, but several other trucks in Chandler's "Bigfoot" series are quite successful in monster truck championships.

Bigfoot 5

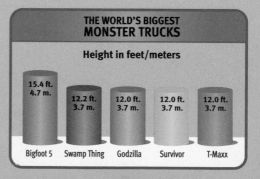

THE WORLD'S BIGGEST MONSTER TRUCKS

Height in feet/meters

Bigfoot 5	Swamp Thing	Godzilla	Survivor	T-Maxx
15.4 ft. 4.7 m.	12.2 ft. 3.7 m.	12.0 ft. 3.7 m.	12.0 ft. 3.7 m.	12.0 ft. 3.7 m.

World's Fastest
Passenger Train

MagLev

The super speedy MagLev train in China carries passengers from Pudong financial district to Pudong International Airport at an average speed of 243 miles (391 km) per hour. The train reaches a top speed of 267 miles (430 km) per hour about 4 minutes into the 8-minute trip. The MagLev, which is short for magnet levitation, actually floats in the air just above the track. Tiny magnets are used to suspend the train, and larger ones are used to pull it forward. The $1.2 billion German-built train system took about 2 years to build and began commercial operation in 2004.

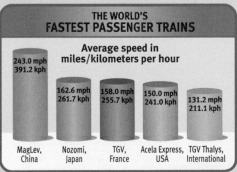

THE WORLD'S
FASTEST PASSENGER TRAINS

Average speed in
miles/kilometers per hour

MagLev, China	Nozomi, Japan	TGV, France	Acela Express, USA	TGV Thalys, International
243.0 mph 391.2 kph	162.6 mph 261.7 kph	158.0 mph 255.7 kph	150.0 mph 241.0 kph	131.2 mph 211.1 kph

43

Country with the Most Telephones

Bermuda

The small island of Bermuda has a lot of telephones! For every 10 people in the country, there are almost 9 phones. That's six times higher than the world average. One reason the people of Bermuda need to stay connected around the island, as well as overseas, is the country's successful tourism industry. Travelers make use of the island's many hotel phones. Bermuda's strong international business sector uses the extensive communication system to keep in contact with companies around the globe.

COUNTRIES WITH THE MOST TELEPHONES

Telephones per 100 inhabitants

Bermuda	Luxembourg	Sweden	Norway	Denmark
87.7	76.8	73.2	73.0	66.7

44

Country with the Most
Cell Phone Users

Luxembourg

COUNTRIES WITH THE
MOST CELL PHONE USERS

Cell phone users per 100 people

Luxembourg	Italy	Israel	Iceland	Sweden
102.0	96.3	95.5	90.6	88.9

In Luxembourg, there are 102 cell phone users per every 100 people. Almost the entire population is taking advantage of wireless communication, with some people having more than one cell phone account. Luxembourg's healthy economy and growing business and financial sectors thrive on the ability to communicate instantly. SES Global—the world's largest satellite company—is located in Luxembourg and provides cell phone services to 94 million people throughout Europe.

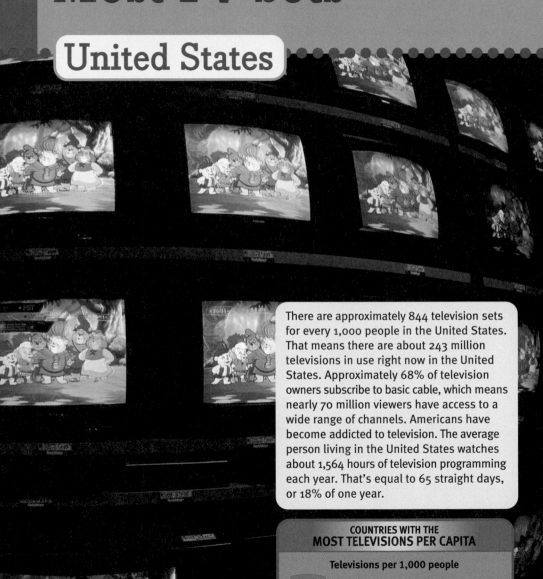

Country with the
Most TV Sets

United States

There are approximately 844 television sets for every 1,000 people in the United States. That means there are about 243 million televisions in use right now in the United States. Approximately 68% of television owners subscribe to basic cable, which means nearly 70 million viewers have access to a wide range of channels. Americans have become addicted to television. The average person living in the United States watches about 1,564 hours of television programming each year. That's equal to 65 straight days, or 18% of one year.

COUNTRIES WITH THE
MOST TELEVISIONS PER CAPITA

Televisions per 1,000 people

USA	Denmark	Latvia	Japan	Australia
844	776	757	719	716

Country with the Highest
Internet Use

Sweden

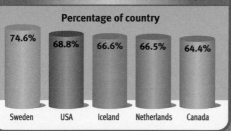

**COUNTRIES WITH THE
HIGHEST PER CAPITA INTERNET USE**

Percentage of country

Sweden	USA	Iceland	Netherlands	Canada
74.6%	68.8%	66.6%	66.5%	64.4%

Sweden is the most connected country in the world with almost 75% of the population accessing the Internet. That means that about 6.7 million Swedes log on to send e-mail and instant messages, shop, and access information. Sweden also has the world's highest percentage of women on-line with 46%, and the highest percentage of people 55 and older on-line with 20%. The Internet is making its way into Swedish classrooms as well. Almost three-quarters of school computers can access on-line information.

Country with the Most
Internet Users

The United States

In the United States, more than 199 million people are surfing the World Wide Web. That's more than 50% of the population. The top four on-line activities in 2004 were e-mail and instant messaging, Web surfing, shopping, and accessing entertainment information. Throughout the nation, the largest number of Internet users is women between the ages of 18 and 54, closely followed by men in that age group. Teens ages 12 to 17 are the third-largest Internet-using group. The average Internet user spends about 15 hours on-line per week.

COUNTRIES WITH THE MOST INTERNET USERS

Users in millions

Country	Users
USA	199.8 M
China	87.0 M
Japan	66.7 M
Germany	47.2 M
UK	34.8 M

World's Most-Visited Web Site

Yahoo!—which stands for Yet Another Hierarchical Officious Oracle—is the world's top Web site, averaging more than 115 million unique users each month. Yahoo! was founded by David Filo and Jerry Yang in 1994 as the first on-line navigational guide to the Internet, and has been expanding ever since. Today users in 25 countries can access Yahoo!'s mail, messenger, calendars, chats, greetings, clubs, and photos in 13 languages. Each day Yahoo! pulls up more than 2.4 billion Web pages for its users.

THE WEB SITES WITH THE MOST VISITORS

Number of new users each month, in millions

Yahoo!	MSN	Time Warner Network	Google	eBay
115.3 M	113.8 M	108.8 M	63.7 M	58.3 M

World's Most-Used Internet Search Engine

Google

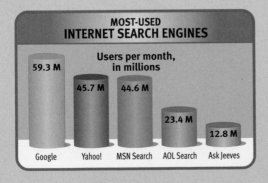

MOST-USED INTERNET SEARCH ENGINES

Users per month, in millions

Google	Yahoo!	MSN Search	AOL Search	Ask Jeeves
59.3 M	45.7 M	44.6 M	23.4 M	12.8 M

Internet users turn to the Google Web site to find out what they need to know. More than 59 million people search the site each month. Google, which is a wordplay of googol—the mathematical word for 1 followed by 100 zeros—certainly seems to live up to its name. It can search more than 4 billion Web pages and 880 million images. More than 81 million new users log on to Google each month, and the giant search engine can display results in 35 languages. Google was created by college students Larry Page and Sergey Brin, and was first accessed by Internet users in 1998.

Country with the Most
Computers-in-Use

The United States

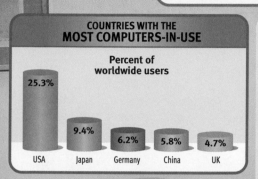

COUNTRIES WITH THE MOST COMPUTERS-IN-USE

Percent of worldwide users

25.3%	9.4%	6.2%	5.8%	4.7%
USA	Japan	Germany	China	UK

The United States is computer crazy—more than one-quarter of the world's computer users live here! There are about 225 million computers in the United States. Americans use computers for business and school, to pay bills, send e-mail, and play games. Surfing the World Wide Web is also a popular American pastime. In the next few years, there will be 64 million households connected to the Internet. Many Americans are also shopping on-line and will spend an estimated $48 billion in 2005.

World's Best-Selling
Kids' Video Game

Madden NFL 2005

Sports fans made Madden NFL 2005 the top-selling kids' video game of 2004 with 5.2 million copies sold. Madden NFL offered gamers some exciting new graphics and features with this edition, which covers the 2004–2005 NFL season. Using Create-a-Fan, players can put themselves into the stands to support their team. Players can also send their teams to training camps to practice their skills before taking the field. And, once ready for competition, players can go on-line to find opponents around the country.

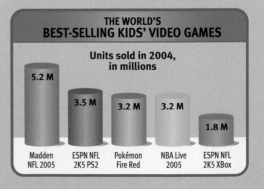

THE WORLD'S BEST-SELLING KIDS' VIDEO GAMES

Units sold in 2004, in millions

Madden NFL 2005	ESPN NFL 2K5 PS2	Pokémon Fire Red	NBA Live 2005	ESPN NFL 2K5 XBox
5.2 M	3.5 M	3.2 M	3.2 M	1.8 M

World's Largest
Optical Telescopes

Keck I/Keck II

The Keck Observatory, located at the top of Mauna Kea in Hawaii, houses two giant optical telescopes—each with a 32.8-foot (10-m) aperture, or opening. Keck I was built in 1992, and Keck II was completed in 1996. Both telescopes stand 8 stories high and weigh 300 tons (272 t). Each telescope contains a primary mirror that measures 33 feet (10 m) in diameter. The telescopes are powerful enough to identify objects about the size of a penny at a distance of more than 5 miles (8 km) away. Astronomers use these giant machines to search for new planetary systems and study parts of the universe that were previously unobservable.

THE WORLD'S
LARGEST OPTICAL TELESCOPES

Aperture in feet/meters

Keck I, Hawaii	Keck II, Hawaii	Hobby-Eberly, Texas	Subaru, Hawaii	Antu, Chile
32.8 ft. 10.0 m.	32.8 ft. 10.0 m.	30.1 ft. 9.2 m.	27.2 ft. 8.3 m.	26.9 ft. 8.2 m.

World's Oldest Astronaut

John Glenn

At age 77, John Glenn returned to space on October 29, 1998 aboard the STS-95 *Discovery* on a nine-day mission. The mission made 134 Earth orbits and traveled 3.6 million miles (5.8 million km). One of the main parts of the mission was to study space flight and its affect on the aging process. Glenn took his first space flight in 1962 aboard the *Mercury-Atlas 6*. Since his first involvement with the space program, Glenn has been a colonel in the Marines and a U.S. Senator.

THE WORLD'S OLDEST ASTRONAUTS

Age at last flight

John Glenn, USA	F. Story Musgrave, USA	Vance D. Brand, USA	Jean-Loup Chretien, France	Valery V. Ryumin, Russia
77	61	59	59	58

World's
Youngest Astronaut

Gherman Titov became the youngest cosmonaut to travel into space when he made his only voyage on August 6, 1961, at the age of 25. Flying aboard the *Vostok 2* spacecraft, Titov completed 17.5 orbits, which lasted 1 day, 1 hour, and 18 minutes. During his time in space, he attempted several activities—including exercising, eating, and sleeping—which astronauts today do automatically. Once he returned to Earth, scientists studied the effects that weightlessness may have had on him.

Gherman Titov

THE WORLD'S
YOUNGEST ASTRONAUTS

Age at first flight

25	26	26	27	27
Gherman S. Titov, Soviet Union	Valentina V. Tereshkova, Soviet Union	Boris B. Yegorov, Soviet Union	Yuri A. Gagarin, Soviet Union	Helen P. Sharman, Britain

Planet with the
Hottest Surface

Venus

THE SOLAR SYSTEM'S HOTTEST PLANETS

Average daytime temperature in Fahrenheit/Celsius

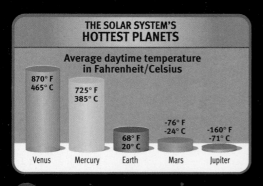

870° F
465° C

725° F
385° C

68° F
20° C

-76° F
-24° C

-160° F
-71° C

Venus | Mercury | Earth | Mars | Jupiter

The surface temperature on Venus can reach a sizzling 870° Fahrenheit (465° C). That's about 19 times hotter than the average temperature on Earth. About every 19 months, Venus is closer to Earth than any other planet in the solar system. Venus is covered by a cloudy, dense atmosphere. This cloud makes it difficult to know what features are on its surface. The atmosphere also reflects a great deal of sunlight. At times, Venus is the third-brightest object in the sky, after the Sun and the Moon.

Planet with the
Most Rings

Saturn

Scientists estimate that approximately 1,000 rings circle Saturn—hundreds more than any other planet. This ring system is only about 328 feet (100 m) thick, but reaches a diameter of 167,780 miles (270,000 km). The three major rings around the planet are named A, B, and C. Although they appear solid, Saturn's rings are made of particles of planet and satellite matter that range in size from about 1 to 15 feet (.3 to 4.5 m). Saturn, which is the sixth planet from the Sun, is the solar system's second-largest planet in size and mass.

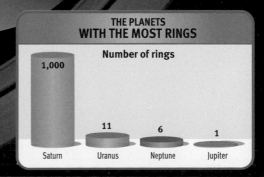

THE PLANETS
WITH THE MOST RINGS

Number of rings

Saturn	Uranus	Neptune	Jupiter
1,000	11	6	1

Planet with the
Most Moons

Jupiter

Jupiter—the fifth planet from the Sun—has 62 moons. Most of these moons—also called satellites—do not resemble traditional moons. Most are quite small, measuring from just .62 miles (.99 km) to 4 miles (6.4 km) across. The moons travel in an elliptical, or egg-shaped, orbit in the opposite direction that Jupiter rotates. Astronomers believe these irregular moons formed somewhere else in the solar system and were pulled into Jupiter's atmosphere when they passed too close to the planet. Astronomers are constantly finding new moons for several of the planets, partly because of the highly sensitive telescopes and cameras now available to them. In fact, during 2004 alone, astronomers discovered four new moons orbiting Jupiter.

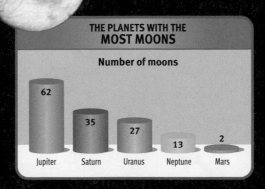

THE PLANETS WITH THE MOST MOONS

Number of moons

Jupiter	Saturn	Uranus	Neptune	Mars
62	35	27	13	2

Planet with the
Fastest Orbit

Mercury

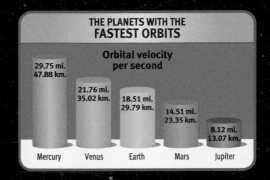

THE PLANETS WITH THE FASTEST ORBITS

Orbital velocity per second

Mercury	Venus	Earth	Mars	Jupiter
29.75 mi. 47.88 km.	21.76 mi. 35.02 km.	18.51 mi. 29.79 km.	14.51 mi. 23.35 km.	8.12 mi. 13.07 km.

Mercury orbits the Sun at about 30 miles (48 km) per second. At this astonishing speed, the planet can circle the Sun in about 88 Earth days. On Mercury, a solar day (the time from one sunrise to the next) lasts about 176 Earth days. Even though Mercury is the closest planet to the Sun, the temperature on the planet can change drastically. During the day, it can reach as high as 840° Fahrenheit (448° C), but at night, temperatures can fall to around -300° Fahrenheit (-149° C)!

Planet with the
Largest Moon

Jupiter

Ganymede is the largest moon of both Jupiter and the solar system. It has a radius of 1,635 miles (2,631 km) and a diameter of 3,280 miles (5,626 km). That is almost 2.5 times larger than Earth's moon. The moon is approximately 1.4 million miles (2.25 million km) away from Jupiter and has an orbital period of about seven days. It is probably made up mostly of rock and ice. It also has lava flows, mountains, valleys, and craters. Ganymede has both light and dark areas that give it a textured appearance. Ganymede was discovered by Galileo Galilei and Simon Marius almost 400 years ago.

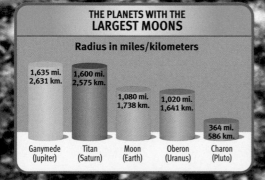

THE PLANETS WITH THE
LARGEST MOONS

Radius in miles/kilometers

Ganymede (Jupiter)	Titan (Saturn)	Moon (Earth)	Oberon (Uranus)	Charon (Pluto)
1,635 mi. 2,631 km.	1,600 mi. 2,575 km.	1,080 mi. 1,738 km.	1,020 mi. 1,641 km.	364 mi. 586 km.

Star That Is
Closest to Earth

Proxima Centauri

Proxima Centauri is approximately 24.7925 trillion miles (39.9233 trillion km) from Earth, making it our closest star other than the Sun. It is the third member of the Alpha Centauri triple system. This tiny red dwarf star is about 10% of the Sun's mass and .006% as bright. The surface temperature is thought to be about 3,000° Fahrenheit (1,650° C). More accurate measures of the star's size are not possible because it is so small. But these measurements are enough to cause scientists to believe that Proxima Centauri does not have any planets orbiting it that support life. If planets did exist, they would be too cold and dark for life-forms to exist.

THE STARS THAT ARE CLOSEST TO EARTH

Distance in trillions of miles/kilometers

Proxima Centauri	Alpha Centauri	Barnard's Star	Wolf 359	Lalande 21185
24.8 T mi. 39.9 T km.	25.6 T mi. 41.2 T km.	35.1 T mi. 56.6 T km.	45.5 T mi. 73.3 T km.	48.3 T mi. 77.8 T km.

World's Largest Asteroid

2001 KX76

2001 KX76

2001 KX76 is the largest asteroid in the universe, measuring at least 744 miles (1,200 km) long. The asteroid is about half the size of Pluto. 2001 KX76 is in the Kuiper belt of asteroids. It is about 4 billion miles (6.5 billion km) from Earth—or roughly 43 times the distance from Earth to the Sun. The asteroid was discovered by analyzing data from some of the world's most powerful virtual and conventional telescopes. Once astronomers were able to verify substantial data about the giant asteroid, it was accepted by the scientific community and is now eligible for a real name. Asteroids do not get permanent names until scientists can prove specific calculations of them. Asteroids in the Kuiper belt traditionally receive a mythological name.

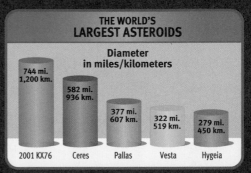

THE WORLD'S LARGEST ASTEROIDS

Diameter in miles/kilometers

Asteroid	Diameter
2001 KX76	744 mi. 1,200 km.
Ceres	582 mi. 936 km.
Pallas	377 mi. 607 km.
Vesta	322 mi. 519 km.
Hygeia	279 mi. 450 km.

Planet with the
Longest Year

Pluto

If you think a year on planet Earth is a long time, don't travel to Pluto any time soon! One year on Pluto is equivalent to 247.7 years on Earth, which means that a single day on Pluto is equal to 6.4 days on Earth. This is because Pluto's location ranges from 2.8 to 4.6 billion miles (4.4 to 7.4 billion km) away from the Sun, approximately 39 times farther from the Sun than Earth. Pluto is also the least massive planet in the solar system. Pluto's gravity is 8% of that on Earth, so that if a 75-pound (34-kg) kid were to be weighed on Pluto, he or she would weigh only 6 pounds (2.7 kg).

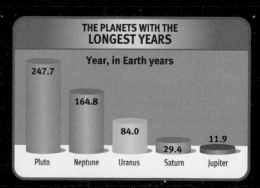

THE PLANETS WITH THE LONGEST YEARS

Year, in Earth years

Pluto	Neptune	Uranus	Saturn	Jupiter
247.7	164.8	84.0	29.4	11.9

Solar System's
Largest Planet

Jupiter

Jupiter has a radius of 43,441 miles (69,909 km)—that's almost 11 times larger than Earth's radius. Jupiter is about 480 million miles (772 million km) from the Sun. It takes almost 12 Earth years for Jupiter to make one complete circle around the Sun. Although it is very large, Jupiter has a high rotation speed. In fact, one Jupiter day is less than 10 Earth hours long. That is the shortest day in the solar system.

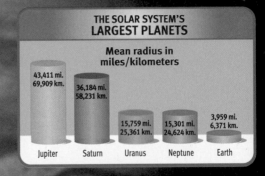

THE SOLAR SYSTEM'S LARGEST PLANETS

Mean radius in miles/kilometers

Jupiter	Saturn	Uranus	Neptune	Earth
43,411 mi. 69,909 km.	36,184 mi. 58,231 km.	15,759 mi. 25,361 km.	15,301 mi. 24,624 km.	3,959 mi. 6,371 km.

Solar System's
Smallest Planet

Pluto

Pluto has a radius of about 707 miles (1,138 km). That's about two-thirds the size of the Moon. Pluto is also the coldest planet, with an average surface temperature of -370° Fahrenheit (-233° Celsius). The planet appears to have polar ice caps that extend halfway to its equator. It is normally the farthest planet from the Sun, but its unusual orbit brings it closer than Neptune about every 250 years. The last time this happened was in 1979, when Pluto became the eighth planet for 20 years. First noticed in 1930, Pluto was the last planet to be discovered in our solar system.

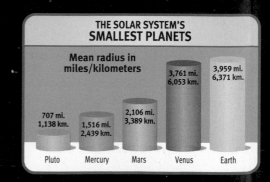

THE SOLAR SYSTEM'S
SMALLEST PLANETS

Mean radius in miles/kilometers

	3,761 mi. 6,053 km.	3,959 mi. 6,371 km.
707 mi. 1,138 km.		2,106 mi. 3,389 km.		
	1,516 mi. 2,439 km.			
Pluto	Mercury	Mars	Venus	Earth

Pluto and its moon, Charon

Sports Records

Football • Baseball • Basketball
Figure Skating • Tennis • Golf • Soccer
Car Racing • Bicycling • Olympics • Hockey

Highest Career
Rushing Total

Emmitt Smith

Running back Emmitt Smith holds the record for all-time rushing yards with 18,355. Smith began his career with the Dallas Cowboys in 1990 and played with the team until the end of the 2002 season. In 2003, Smith signed a two-year contract with the Arizona Cardinals. Smith also holds the NFL records for the most carries with 4,142 and the most rushing touchdowns with 164. He retired from the NFL in 2004.

PLAYERS WITH THE
HIGHEST CAREER RUSHING TOTALS

Rushing yards

Emmitt Smith, 1990–2004	Walter Payton, 1975–1987	Barry Sanders, 1989–1999	Eric Dickerson, 1983–1993	Tony Dorsett, 1977–1988
18,355	16,726	15,269	13,259	12,739

Quarterback with the
Most Passing Yards

Dan Marino

During his seventeen-year career, Dan Marino has racked up 61,361 passing yards. Marino was selected by the Dolphins as the 27th pick in the first-round draft in 1983. He remained a Dolphin for the rest of his career, setting many impressive records. Marino has the most career pass attempts (8,358), the most career completions (4,967), the most career touchdown passes (420), the most passing yards in a season (5,084), and the most seasons leading the league in completions (6). Marino retired from the NFL in 2000.

**PLAYERS WITH THE
MOST PASSING YARDS**

Yards

Dan Marino, 1983–2000	John Elway, 1983–1999	Brett Favre, 1991–	Warren Moon, 1984–2000	Fran Tarkenton, 1961–1978
61,361	51,475	49,734	49,325	47,003

Most Single-Season Touchdowns

Priest Holmes

In a game against the Chicago Bears in December 2003, Priest Holmes scored his twenty-sixth and twenty-seventh touchdowns of the season. By doing this, Holmes broke the record for total touchdowns in a single season, and the record for rushing touchdowns in a single season. The two-time Pro Bowl running back began his professional career with the Baltimore Ravens in 1997, and later signed with the Kansas City Chiefs in 2001. Holmes was named NFL Offensive Player of the Year in 2002. He was voted the Chiefs' Most Valuable Player that same year and also named the team's offensive captain.

PLAYERS WITH THE MOST SINGLE-SEASON TOUCHDOWNS

Touchdowns scored

Priest Holmes, 2003	Marshall Faulk, 2000	Emmitt Smith, 1995	John Riggins, 1983	Terrell Davis, 1998
27	26	25	24	23

Most Career Touchdowns

Jerry Rice

With a career record of 207 touchdowns, Jerry Rice is widely considered to be one of the greatest wide receivers ever to play in the National Football League. He holds a total of 14 NFL records, including career receptions (1,549), receiving yards (22,895), receiving touchdowns (197), consecutive 100-catch seasons (4), most games with 100 receiving yards (73), and many others. He was named NFL Player of the Year twice, *Sports Illustrated* Player of the Year four times, and NFL Offensive Player of the Year once.

PLAYERS WITH THE MOST CAREER TOUCHDOWNS

Touchdowns scored

Jerry Rice, 1985–	Emmitt Smith, 1990–2004	Marcus Allen, 1982–1996	Marshall Faulk, 1994–	Cris Carter, 1987–2003
207	175	145	135	130

Team with the Most
Super Bowl Wins

Cowboys and 49ers

The Dallas Cowboys and the San Francisco 49ers have each won a total of five Super Bowl championships. The first championship win for the Cowboys was in 1972, which was followed by wins in 1978, 1993, 1994, and 1996. Out of those 10 victories, the game with the most spectators was Super Bowl XXVII, when Dallas defeated the Buffalo Bills at the Rose Bowl in Pasadena, California, in 1993. The 49ers had their first win in 1982, and repeated their victory in 1985, 1989, 1990, and 1995.

TEAMS WITH THE MOST SUPER BOWL WINS

Super Bowls won

Dallas Cowboys	San Francisco 49ers	Pittsburgh Steelers	Green Bay Packers	Washington Redskins
5	5	4	3	3

Highest Career
Scoring Total

Gary Anderson

Gary Anderson is the NFL's top kicker. Altogether he scored 2,434 points in his 23 seasons of professional play. In 1998, Anderson hit 35-of-35 field goals and became the first NFL player to go an entire season without missing a kick. Anderson began his career with the Pittsburgh Steelers in 1982 and later played with the Philadelphia Eagles and the San Francisco 49ers. He joined the Vikings in 1998 and scored 542 points for them—the fifth-highest in team history. Anderson joined the Tennessee Titans in 2003 and played for two seasons before retiring.

PLAYERS WITH THE
HIGHEST CAREER SCORING TOTALS

Points scored

Gary Anderson, 1982–2005	Morten Andersen, 1980–	George Blanda, 1949–1975	Norm Johnson, 1983–1999	Nick Lowery, 1978–1996
2,434	2,358	2,002	1,736	1,711

Biggest
Super Bowl Blowout

Super Bowl XXIV

On January 28, 1990, the San Francisco 49ers beat the Denver Broncos by a score of 55 to 10 during Super Bowl XXIV. Some 73,000 fans crowded into the Louisiana Superdome to see San Francisco score the most points in Super Bowl history. 49ers quarterback Joe Montana was named Super Bowl MVP for the third time, completing 22 out of 29 passes. San Francisco over-powered Denver in first downs (28 to 12) as well as net yards (461 to 167.)

BIGGEST
SUPER BOWL BLOWOUTS

Point difference

45	36	35	32	29
49ers vs. Broncos 1990	Bears vs. Patriots 1986	Cowboys vs. Bills 1993	Redskins vs. Broncos 1988	Los Angeles vs. Redskins 1984

Top-Winning NFL Coach

Don Shula

During his 33 years as a head coach in the National Football League, Don Shula led his teams to a remarkable 347 wins. When Shula became head coach of the Baltimore Colts in 1963, he became the youngest head coach in football history. He stayed with the team until 1969 and reached the playoffs four times. Shula became the head coach for the Miami Dolphins in 1970 and coached them until 1995. After leading them to Super Bowl wins in 1972 and 1973, Shula became one of only five coaches to win the championship in back-to-back years.

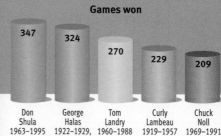

TOP-WINNING NFL COACHES

Games won

Don Shula 1963–1995	George Halas 1922–1929, 1933–1941, 1946–1955, 1958–1967	Tom Landry 1960–1988	Curly Lambeau 1919–1957	Chuck Noll 1969–1991
347	324	270	229	209

World's Largest
NFL Stadium

FedEx Field

WORLD'S LARGEST
NFL STADIUMS

Seating capacity

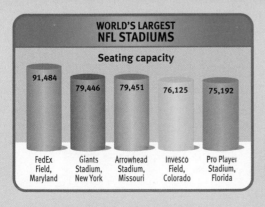

FedEx Field, Maryland	Giants Stadium, New York	Arrowhead Stadium, Missouri	Invesco Field, Colorado	Pro Player Stadium, Florida
91,484	79,446	79,451	76,125	75,192

FedEx Field in Maryland is home to the Washington Redskins and can accommodate 91,484 of their fans. The stadium has undergone four expansions since it opened in 1997. With all this room, the Redskins have led the NFL in attendance for the last four seasons. Spectators who really want their space can buy a luxury suite at midfield for about $160,000. There, fans have access to a restroom, refrigerator, television, and lounge area. The natural turf field has more than 4 miles (6.4 km) of heated tubing beneath the grass to keep it from freezing.

World's All-Time
Home Run Hitter

Hank Aaron

In 1974, Hank Aaron broke Babe Ruth's lifetime record of 714 home runs. By the time he retired from baseball in 1976, Aaron had hit a total of 755 homers— a record that has remained unbroken. His amazing hitting ability earned him the nickname "Hammerin' Hank." Aaron holds many other distinguished baseball records, including most lifetime runs batted in (2,297) and most years with 30 or more home runs (15). Aaron was an excellent defensive player, earning three Gold Glove Awards.

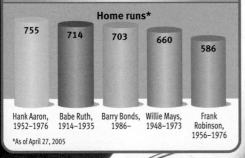

THE WORLD'S TOP 5
ALL-TIME HOME RUN HITTERS

Home runs*

755	714	703	660	586
Hank Aaron, 1952–1976	Babe Ruth, 1914–1935	Barry Bonds, 1986–	Willie Mays, 1948–1973	Frank Robinson, 1956–1976

*As of April 27, 2005

Highest Seasonal
Home Run Total

Barry Bonds

**BASEBALL'S TOP SEASONAL
HOME RUN HITTERS**

Number of home runs

Barry Bonds, 2001	Mark McGwire, 1998	Sammy Sosa, 1998	Mark McGwire, 1999	Sammy Sosa, 2001
73	70	66	65	64

Barry Bonds smashed Mark McGwire's record for seasonal home runs when he hit his 71st home run on October 5, 2001, in the first inning of a game against the Los Angeles Dodgers. Two innings later, he hit number 72. Bonds, a left fielder for the San Francisco Giants, has a career total of 668 home runs. He also holds the records for seasonal walks (198) and seasonal on-base percentage (0.582). Bonds and his father, hitting coach Bobby Bonds, hold the all-time father-son home run record with 954.

Most
Career Hits

Pete Rose

During his 23 years of professional baseball, Rose belted an amazing 4,256 hits. He got his record-setting hit in 1985, when he was a player-manager for the Cincinnati Reds. By the time Pete Rose retired as a player from Major League Baseball in 1986, he had set several other career records. Rose holds the Major League records for the most career games (3,562), the most times at bat (14,053), and the most seasons with more than 200 hits (10). During his career, he played for the Cincinnati Reds, the Philadelphia Phillies, and the Montreal Expos.

PLAYERS WITH THE MOST CAREER HITS

Hits

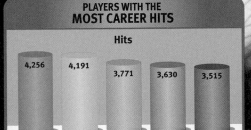

Pete Rose, 1963–1986	Ty Cobb, 1905–1928	Hank Aaron, 1952–1976	Stan Musial, 1941–1963	Tris Speaker, 1907–1928
4,256	4,191	3,771	3,630	3,515

Most
Career Strikeouts

Nolan Ryan

Nolan Ryan, a right-handed pitcher from Refugio, Texas, leads Major League Baseball with an incredible 5,714 career strikeouts. In his impressive 28-year career, he played for the New York Mets, the California Angels, the Houston Astros, and the Texas Rangers. Ryan led the American League in strikeouts 10 times. In 1989, at the age of 42, Ryan became the oldest pitcher ever to lead the Major League in strikeouts. Ryan set another record in 1991 when he pitched his seventh career no-hitter.

PLAYERS WITH THE
MOST CAREER STRIKEOUTS

Strikeouts

5,714	4,349	4,195	4,136	3,701
Nolan Ryan, 1966–1993	Roger Clemens, 1984–	Randy Johnson, 1989–	Steve Carlton, 1965–1988	Bert Blyleven, 1970–1992

*As of April 28, 2005

Highest Seasonal
Batting Average

Rogers Hornsby

Rogers Hornsby is widely considered by most people to be Major League Baseball's greatest right-handed hitter. In 1924, he had a record-setting season batting average of .424. More than 75 years later, his record still stands. From 1921 to 1925—playing for the St. Louis Cardinals—Hornsby hit an average of .401. And during three of those seasons, he hit above .400. Hornsby's major league lifetime batting average is an incredible .358, which is the second-highest career average in the history of the league after Ty Cobb. Hornsby was inducted to the Baseball Hall of Fame in 1942.

**PLAYERS WITH THE
HIGHEST SEASONAL BATTING AVERAGES**

Season average

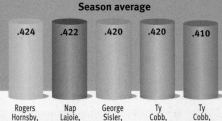

.424	.422	.420	.420	.410
Rogers Hornsby, 1924	Nap Lajoie, 1901	George Sisler, 1922	Ty Cobb, 1911	Ty Cobb, 1912

Baseball Player with the Most Expensive Contract

Alex Rodriguez

In 2001, shortstop Alex Rodriguez signed a ten-year deal with the Texas Rangers for $252 million. This does not include any bonuses he may earn for winning titles or awards, or any money he could make from potential endorsements. The right-hander began his career with Seattle in 1994 and quickly became a respected player. He became the fourth shortstop ever to lead the league in home runs. In 2004, Rodriguez joined the New York Yankees, and the ball club is now responsible for paying the majority of his contract.

BASEBALL PLAYERS WITH THE MOST EXPENSIVE CONTRACTS

Yearly salary in millions of US dollars

Player	Salary
Alex Rodriguez, New York Yankees	$25.2 M
Manny Ramirez, Boston Red Sox	$20.0 M
Derek Jeter, New York Yankees	$18.9 M
Roger Clemens, Houston Astros	$18.0 M
Barry Bonds, San Francisco Giants	$18.0 M

Most MVP Awards in the National League

Barry Bonds

Barry Bonds of the San Francisco Giants has earned an amazing seven Most Valuable Player awards for his outstanding athleticism in the National Baseball League. He received his first two MVP awards in 1990 and 1992 while playing for the Pittsburgh Pirates. The next five awards came while wearing the Giants uniform in 1993, 2001, 2002, 2003, and 2004. Bonds is the first player to win an MVP award three times in consecutive seasons. In fact, Bonds is the only baseball player in history to have won more than three MVP awards.

PLAYERS WITH THE MOST NATIONAL LEAGUE MVP AWARDS

Most Valuable Player (MVP) awards

Player	MVP awards
Barry Bonds, 1986–	7
Roy Campanella, 1948–1957	3
Stan Musial, 1941–1963	3
Mike Schmidt, 1972–1989	3
Ernie Banks, 1953–1971	2

Most MVP Awards in the
American League

Yogi Berra, Joe DiMaggio, Jimmie Foxx, and Mickey Mantle each won three Most Valuable Player awards during their professional careers in the American Baseball League. DiMaggio, Berra, and Mantle were all New York Yankees. Foxx played for the Athletics, the Cubs, and the Phillies. The player with the biggest gap between wins was DiMaggio, who won his first award in 1939 and his last in 1947. Also nicknamed "Joltin' Joe" and the "Yankee Clipper," DiMaggio began playing in the major leagues in 1936. The following year, he led the league in home runs and runs scored. He was elected to the Baseball Hall of Fame in 1955.

Yogi Berra, Joe DiMaggio, Jimmie Foxx, and Mickey Mantle

PLAYERS WITH THE MOST
AMERICAN LEAGUE MVP AWARDS

Most Valuable Player (MVP) awards

Yogi Berra, 1946–1963; 1965	Joe DiMaggio, 1936–1951	Jimmie Foxx, 1925–1945	Mickey Mantle, 1951–1960	Juan Gonzalez, 1989–
3	3	3	3	2

Mickey Mantle

Most Cy Young Awards

Roger Clemens

Houston Astros starting pitcher Roger Clemens has earned a record seven Cy Young awards during his career so far. He set a Major League record in April 1986 when he struck out 20 batters in one game. He later tied this record in September 1996. In September 2001, Clemens became the first Major League pitcher to win 20 of his first 21 decisions in one season. In June 2003, he became the first pitcher in more than a decade to win his 300th game. He also struck out his 4,000th batter that year.

PITCHERS WITH THE MOST CY YOUNG AWARDS

Cy Young Awards

Roger Clemens, 1984–	Randy Johnson, 1988–	Steve Carlton, 1965–1988	Greg Maddux, 1986–	Sandy Koufax, 1955–1966
7	5	4	4	3

Team with the Most
World Series Wins

New York Yankees

The New York Yankees were the World Series champions a record 26 times between 1923 and 2000. The team picked up their latest win in October of 2000 when they beat the New York Mets. The Yankees beat the Mets four games to one to win their third consecutive championship. Since their early days, the team has included some of baseball's greatest players, including Babe Ruth, Lou Gehrig, Yogi Berra, Joe DiMaggio, and Mickey Mantle.

TEAMS WITH THE MOST
WORLD SERIES WINS

Wins

Team	Wins
NY Yankees, 1923–2000	26
St. Louis Cardinals, 1926–1982	9
Philadelphia/ Kansas City/ Oakland Athletics, 1910–1989	9
Brooklyn/ LA Dodgers, 1955–1988	6
NY/ San Francisco Giants, 1905–1954	5

Player with the Most Career RBIs

Hank Aaron

Right-handed Hank Aaron batted in an incredible 2,297 runs during his 23 years in the major leagues. Aaron began his professional career with the Indianapolis Clowns, a team in the Negro American League, in 1952. He was traded to the Atlanta Braves in 1956 and won the National League batting championship with an average of .328. He was named the league's Most Valuable Player a year later when he led his team to a World Series victory. Aaron retired as a player in 1976 and was inducted into the Baseball Hall of Fame in 1982.

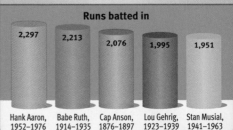

PLAYERS WITH THE MOST CAREER RBIs

Runs batted in

Hank Aaron, 1952–1976	Babe Ruth, 1914–1935	Cap Anson, 1876–1897	Lou Gehrig, 1923–1939	Stan Musial, 1941–1963
2,297	2,213	2,076	1,995	1,951

Player with the
Most At Bats

Pete Rose

With 14,053 at bats, Pete Rose has stood behind the plate more than any other Major League player. Rose signed with the Cincinnati Reds after graduating high school in 1963 and played second base. During his impressive career, Rose set several other records including most singles in the Major Leagues (3,315), most seasons with 600 or more at bats in the major league (17), most career doubles in the National League (746), and most career runs in the National League (2,165). He was also named World Series MVP, Sports Illustrated Sportsman of the Year, and The Sporting News Man of the Year.

PLAYERS WITH THE
MOST AT BATS

At bats

14,053	12,364	11,988	11,551	11,434
Pete Rose	Hank Aaron	Carl Yastrzanski	Cal Ripken, Jr.	Ty Cobb

Player Who Played the Most
Consecutive Games

Cal Ripken, Jr.

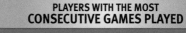

**PLAYERS WITH THE MOST
CONSECUTIVE GAMES PLAYED**

Consecutive games played

2,632	2,130	1,307	1,207	1,117
Cal Ripken, Jr., 1978–2001	Lou Gehrig, 1923–1939	Everett Scott, 1914–1925	Steve Garvey, 1968–1988	Billy Williams, 1959–1974

Cal Ripken, Jr., a right-handed third baseman for the Baltimore Orioles, played 2,632 consecutive games from May 30, 1982, to September 20, 1998. He also holds the record for the most consecutive innings played: 8,243. In June 1996, Ripken also broke the world record for consecutive games with 2,216, surpassing Sachio Kinugasa of Japan. When he played as a shortstop, Ripken set Major League records for most home runs (345) and most extra base hits (855) for his position. He has started in the All-Star Game a record 19 times in a row.

Country with the Most Little League
Championship Wins

United States

2004 Little League World Series U.S. semifinals

COUNTRIES WITH THE MOST
LITTLE LEAGUE CHAMPIONSHIP WINS

Number of wins

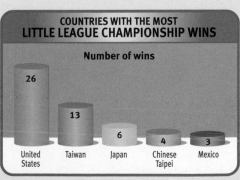

United States	Taiwan	Japan	Chinese Taipei	Mexico
26	13	6	4	3

The United States has won the most Little League Championships with 26 victories. The first Championship was held in 1947 and was extremely popular. The publicity from this game helped turn Little League baseball into the world's largest organized sports program. It was founded in Pennsylvania in 1939 with three teams and has grown to include more than 180,000 teams and 35 million participants in more than 100 countries. The Championship is held the weekend before Labor Day in Williamsport, Pennsylvania.

89

Men's Basketball Team with the Most NCAA Championships

UCLA

The University of California, Los Angeles (UCLA) has won the NCAA Basketball Championship a record 11 times. The Bruins won their 11th championship in 1995. The school has won 23 of their last 41 league titles and has been in the NCAA playoffs for 35 of the last 41 years. Not surprisingly, UCLA has produced some basketball legends, too, including Kareem Abdul-Jabbar, Reggie Miller, and Baron Davis. For the last 36 years, the Bruins have called Pauley Pavilion home.

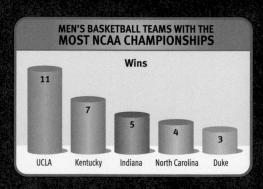

MEN'S BASKETBALL TEAMS WITH THE MOST NCAA CHAMPIONSHIPS

Wins

Team	Wins
UCLA	11
Kentucky	7
Indiana	5
North Carolina	4
Duke	3

Women's Basketball Team with the
Most NCAA Championships

Tennessee

WOMEN'S BASKETBALL TEAMS WITH THE MOST NCAA CHAMPIONSHIPS

Wins

6	5	2	2	2
University of Tennessee	University of Connecticut	Louisiana Tech	Stanford University	University of Southern California

The Tennessee Lady Volunteers, or Lady Vols as they are known, have won six NCAA basketball championships. Their latest win occurred in 1998, when the Lady Vols had a perfect record of 39–0, which was the most seasonal wins ever in women's collegiate basketball. In 2004, Tennessee was in the championship but was beaten by the University of Connecticut Huskies. Since 1976, an impressive 14 Lady Vols have been to the Olympics. And five Lady Vols have been inducted into the Women's Basketball Hall of Fame in Knoxville, Tennessee.

91

Highest Career
Scoring Average

Wilt Chamberlain and Michael Jordan

During their legendary careers, both Michael Jordan and Wilt Chamberlain averaged an amazing 30.1 points per game. Jordan played for the Chicago Bulls and the Washington Wizards. He led the league in scoring for seven years. During the 1986 season, he became only the second person ever to score 3,000 points. Chamberlain played for the Philadelphia Warriors, the Philadelphia 76ers, and the Los Angeles Lakers. In addition to the highest scoring average, he also holds the record for the most games with 50 or more points with 118.

Michael Jordan

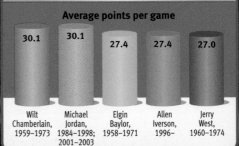

**PLAYERS WITH THE
HIGHEST CAREER SCORING AVERAGES**

Average points per game

30.1	30.1	27.4	27.4	27.0
Wilt Chamberlain, 1959–1973	Michael Jordan, 1984–1998; 2001–2003	Elgin Baylor, 1958–1971	Allen Iverson, 1996–	Jerry West, 1960–1974

Most Career
Games Played

Robert Parish

Robert Parish was a first-round draft pick by the Golden State Warriors in 1976. During his 21-year career, Parish played in a total of 1,611 NBA games. Parish has played in nine NBA All-Star Games and was honored as one of the 50 Greatest Players in NBA History during the 1996–1997 season. He won three championships with the Boston Celtics and one with the Chicago Bulls. By the time he retired in 1997, Parish had scored an astounding 23,334 points and grabbed 14,715 rebounds.

PLAYERS WITH THE
MOST CAREER GAMES PLAYED

Games played

1,611	1,560	1,504	1,476	1,418
Robert Parish, 1976–1997	Kareem Abdul-Jabbar, 1969–1989	John Stockton, 1984–2003	Karl Malone, 1985–2004	Kevin Willis, 1984–

Player with the Most MVP Awards

Kareem Abdul-Jabbar

Considered by most people to be one of the greatest players ever to play basketball, Kareem Abdul-Jabbar has earned six Most Valuable Player Awards. He was also an NBA Finals MVP twice. Abdul-Jabbar, a 7-foot-tall (2.1 m) center, scored double figures in an amazing 787 straight games. During his twenty-year career, this basketball legend played 1,560 games, averaging 24.6 points and 11.2 rebounds a game. He holds many impressive records, including the most blocked shots.

PLAYERS WITH THE MOST MVP AWARDS

MVP awards

Kareem Abdul-Jabbar, 1969–1989	Michael Jordan, 1984–1998, 2001–2003	Bill Russell, 1955–1969	Larry Bird, 1979–1992	Moses Malone, 1974–1994
6	5	4	3	3

NBA's
Largest Arena

The Palace of Auburn Hills

The Palace of Auburn Hills in Michigan can seat an incredible 22,076 people for a Detroit Pistons game. The arena was built in 1988 at a cost of $70 million. It has been awarded "Arena of the Year" by *Performance* magazine seven times. Because of its excellent reputation, The Palace of Auburn Hills has been chosen to host first and second round games during the 2006 NCAA Men's Basketball Championship. It is also home to the Detroit Shock, a WNBA basketball team.

THE NBA'S
LARGEST ARENAS

Seating capacity

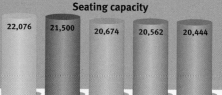

22,076	21,500	20,674	20,562	20,444
The Palace of Auburn Hills, Michigan	United Center, Illinois	MCI Center, Washington, DC	Gund Arena, Ohio	Wachovia Center, Pennsylvania

Most Career
Points

Kareem Abdul-Jabbar

Kareem Abdul-Jabbar scored a total of 38,387 points during his highly successful career. In 1969, Abdul-Jabbar began his NBA tenure with the Milwaukee Bucks. He was named Rookie of the Year in 1970. The following year he scored 2,596 points and helped the Bucks win the NBA championship. He was traded to the Los Angeles Lakers in 1975. With his new team, Abdul-Jabbar won the NBA championship in 1980, 1982, 1985, 1987, and 1988. He retired from basketball in 1989 and was inducted into the Basketball Hall of Fame in 1995.

PLAYERS WITH THE
MOST CAREER POINTS

Points scored

Player	Points scored
Kareem Abdul-Jabbar, 1969–1989	38,387
Karl Malone, 1985–2004	36,928
Michael Jordan, 1984–1998; 2001–2003	32,292
Wilt Chamberlain, 1959–1973	31,419
Moses Malone, 1974–1994	27,409

WNBA Player with the Highest Free Throw Scoring Average

Eva Nemcova

WNBA PLAYERS WITH THE HIGHEST FREE THROW SCORING AVERAGES

Career free throw average

.897	.887	.882	.871	.864
Eva Nemcova, 1997–2001	Sue Bird, 2002–	Elena Tornikidou, 1999–2001	Cynthia Cooper, 1997–	Janeth Arcain, 1997–2004

When Eva Nemcova stood on the free throw line, her shot usually went in. With a free throw average of .897, Nemcova was not a person to foul. The six-foot-three-inch-tall (1.9-m) guard played for the Cleveland Rockers from 1997 to 2001. She was the fourth overall draft pick in the league's inaugural year and was named to the WNBA First Team that season. In 1999, Nemcova became the ninth person in the WNBA to score more than 1,000 points. In 2000, she set a WNBA free throw record when she made 66 consecutive shots that season. Nemcova retired in 2001 after an ACL injury.

97

WNBA Player with the
Most Career Points

Lisa Leslie

As a center for the Los Angeles Sparks, Lisa Leslie has scored 4,215 points. Leslie has a career average of 17.5 points per game. She was named MVP of the WNBA All-Star Games in 1999, 2001, and 2002. Leslie was also a member of the 1996 and 2000 Olympic gold medal-winning women's basketball teams. In both 2001 and 2002, Leslie led her team to victory in the WNBA championship and was named Finals MVP. Leslie set another record on July 30, 2002, when she became the first player in WNBA history to slam dunk in a game.

WNBA PLAYERS WITH THE
MOST CAREER POINTS

Points scored*

Lisa Leslie, 1997–	Tina Thompson, 1997–	Andrea Stinson, 1997–	Katie Smith, 2000–	Sheryl Swoopes, 1997–
4,215	3,699	3,329	3,299	3,280

*As of March 30, 2005

WNBA Player with the Highest
Career PPG Average

Cynthia Cooper

WNBA PLAYERS WITH THE HIGHEST CAREER PPG AVERAGES

Average points per game*

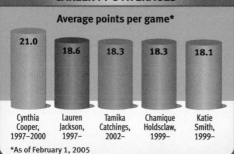

Cynthia Cooper, 1997–2000	Lauren Jackson, 1997–	Tamika Catchings, 2002–	Chamique Holdsclaw, 1999–	Katie Smith, 1999–
21.0	18.6	18.3	18.3	18.1

*As of February 1, 2005

Guard Cynthia Cooper played for the Houston Comets from 1997 to 2000 and averaged 21.0 points per game (PPG). Cooper was a three-time WNBA scoring champion in 1997, 1998, and 1999, and she was the first player in the league to reach the 500, 1,000, 2,000, and 2,500 point marks. She scored 30 or more points in 16 of her 120 games and had a 92-game double-figure scoring streak from 1997 to 2000.

99

Top Male World-Champion
Figure Skaters

Kurt Browning, Scott Hamilton, Hayes Jenkins, and Alexei Yagudin each won 4 world championship competitions. Yagudin is from Russia and won his World Championship titles in 1998, 2000, 2001, and 2002. In the 2001–2002 season, Yagudin became the first male skater to win a gold medal in the four major skating events—Europeans, Grand Prix Final, Worlds, and the Olympics—in the same year. Browning is from Canada and was inducted into the Canadian Sports Hall of Fame in 1994. Hamilton and Jenkins are from the United States. Hamilton won the competitions from 1981 to 1984. He also won a gold medal in the 1984 Olympics. Jenkins's impressive skating career included winning every major championship between 1953 and 1956.

Kurt Browning, Scott Hamilton, Hayes Jenkins, and Alexei Yagudin

Alexei Yagudin

MEN WITH THE MOST
WORLD FIGURE-SKATING CHAMPIONSHIP WINS

World Championship wins

Kurt Browning, Canada, 1989–1993	Scott Hamilton, USA, 1981–1984	Hayes Jenkins, USA, 1953–1956	Alexei Yagudin, Russia, 1998–2002	David Jenkins, USA, 1957–1959
4	4	4	4	3

Top Female World-Champion Figure Skaters

WOMEN WITH THE MOST WORLD FIGURE-SKATING CHAMPIONSHIP WINS

World Championship wins

Carol Heiss, USA 1956–1960	Michelle Kwan, USA, 1996–2003	Katarina Witt, E. Germany, 1984–1988	Sjoukje Dijkstra, Netherlands, 1962–1964	Peggy Fleming, USA, 1966–1968
5	5	4	3	3

Carol Heiss/ Michelle Kwan

Michelle Kwan

American figure skaters Carol Heiss and Michelle Kwan have won the Women's World Figure Skating Championships five times. Heiss, whose wins came between 1956 and 1960, also won an Olympic silver medal for women's figure skating in 1956, and then a gold medal during the 1960 Winter Olympics in Squaw Valley, California. Kwan won the World Championships in 1996, 1998, 2000, 2001, and 2003. Kwan has also won the Women's U.S. Championships a record six times. She picked up a silver medal in the 1998 Olympics and won a bronze in 2002.

World's Top-Earning Male Tennis Player

Pete Sampras

During his 13 years as a professional tennis player, Pete Sampras has earned more than $43 million. That averages out to about $9,060 a day! In addition to being the top-earning male tennis player of all time, Sampras also holds several other titles. He has been named ATP Player of the Year a record six times, he has the most career game wins with 762, and he has been ranked number one for the most weeks with 276. And in 1997, Sampras became the only tennis player to be named U.S. Olympic Committee Sportsman of the Year. Sampras retired from tennis in 2003.

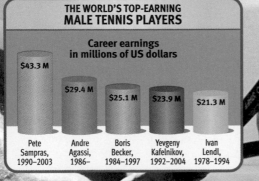

THE WORLD'S TOP-EARNING MALE TENNIS PLAYERS

Career earnings in millions of US dollars

Player	Career earnings
Pete Sampras, 1990–2003	$43.3 M
Andre Agassi, 1986–	$29.4 M
Boris Becker, 1984–1997	$25.1 M
Yevgeny Kafelnikov, 1992–2004	$23.9 M
Ivan Lendl, 1978–1994	$21.3 M

World's Top-Earning Female Tennis Player

Steffi Graf

During her 17-year career, Steffi Graf earned $21.8 million. After turning professional at age 13, Graf scored 902 victories, including 22 Grand Slam singles titles and 107 tournament titles. During her career, she was ranked number one for 377 weeks and named the WTA Player of the Year seven times. Graf's most successful year in tennis came in 1988 when she won 96% of her matches, all four Grand Slam singles titles, and an Olympic gold medal. Graf retired in 1999 and is married to tennis superstar Andre Agassi.

THE WORLD'S TOP-EARNING FEMALE TENNIS PLAYERS

Career earnings in millions of US dollars

Steffi Graf, 1982–1999	Martina Navratilova, 1975–1994	Lindsey Davenport, 1993–	Martina Hingis, 1994–2003	Arantxa Sanchez-Vicario, 1988–2002
$21.8 M	$21.2 M	$18.7 M	$18.3 M	$16.9 M

Man with the Most Singles
Grand Slam Titles

Pete Sampras

Pete Sampras holds the title for the most Grand Slam male singles titles with 14 victories. He has won two Australian Opens, seven Wimbledon titles, and five U.S. Opens between 1990 and 2002. After not winning a major title in two years, Sampras was a surprise victory at the 2002 U.S. Open. He was the number 17 seed and beat Andre Agassi in a three-hour final match. Sampras officially retired from the sport in 2003.

MEN WITH THE MOST
SINGLES GRAND SLAM TITLES

Titles won

Pete Sampras, 1990–2002	Roy Emerson, 1961–1967	Bjorn Borg, 1974–1981	Rod Laver, 1960–1969	Andre Agassi, 1992–
14	12	11	11	8

Woman with the Most Singles Grand Slam Titles

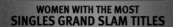

WOMEN WITH THE MOST SINGLES GRAND SLAM TITLES

Titles won

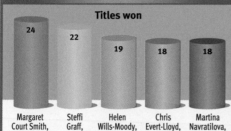

Margaret Court Smith, 1960–1975	Steffi Graff, 1987–1999	Helen Wills-Moody, 1923–1938	Chris Evert-Lloyd, 1974–1986	Martina Navratilova, 1974–1995
24	22	19	18	18

Between 1960 and 1975, Margaret Court Smith won 24 Grand Slam singles titles. She is the only woman ever to win the French, British, U.S., and Australian titles during one year in both the singles and doubles competitions. She was only the second woman to win all four titles in the same year. During her amazing career, she won a total of 66 Grand Slam championships—more than any other woman. Court was the world's top-seeded female player from 1962 to 1965, 1969 to 1970, and 1973. She was inducted into the International Tennis Hall of Fame in 1979.

Margaret Court Smith

PGA Player with the Lowest
Seasonal Average

Vijay Singh

Vijay Singh was the best golfer in the PGA in 2004 with the lowest seasonal average of 68.84. Originally from Fiji, Singh turned professional in 1982 and joined the PGA Tour in 1993. He had his first PGA victory at the Buick Classic that same year. Since then, Singh has won 24 PGA events, including the Masters Tournament, the PGA Championship, and the Honda Classic. Singh has also scored 22 international victories. His career winnings to date total more than $1.1 million.

PGA PLAYERS WITH THE LOWEST SEASONAL AVERAGES

Seasonal average in 2004

Vijay Singh	Ernie Els	Tiger Woods	Phil Mickelson	Retief Goosen
68.84	68.98	69.04	69.16	69.32

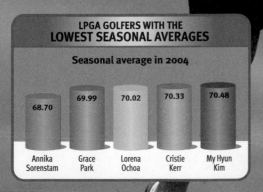

LPGA Golfer with the Lowest
Seasonal Average

Annika Sorenstam

Swedish golfer Annika Sorenstam had the lowest seasonal average in the LPGA in 2004 with 68.70. Sorenstam began her professional career in 1994 and has set or tied 30 LPGA records since then. In 2002, she became the first female player to finish below 69.0 with an average of 68.7. Sorenstam is currently tied for eighth place on the LPGA's career victory list. In 2003, Sorenstam became the first woman in 58 years to compete in a PGA event when she played in the Bank of America Colonial tournament.

LPGA GOLFERS WITH THE LOWEST SEASONAL AVERAGES

Seasonal average in 2004

Annika Sorenstam	Grace Park	Lorena Ochoa	Cristie Kerr	My Hyun Kim
68.70	69.99	70.02	70.33	70.48

Man with the Most Major Tournament Wins

Jack Nicklaus

Jack Nicklaus has won a total of 18 major championships including 6 Masters, 5 PGAs, 4 U.S. Opens, and 3 British Opens. Nicklaus was named PGA Player of the Year five times. He was a member of the winning U.S. Ryder Cup team six times, and was an individual World Cup winner a record three times. He was inducted into the World Golf Hall of Fame in 1974, just 12 years after he turned professional. He joined the U.S. Senior PGA Tour in 1990.

In addition to playing the game, Nicklaus has designed close to 200 golf courses and written a number of popular books about the sport.

MEN WITH THE MOST MAJOR TOURNAMENT WINS

Major tournaments won

18	11	9	9	8
Jack Nicklaus, 1963–1986	Walter Hagen, 1914–1929	Ben Hogan, 1946–1953	Gary Player, 1959–1978	Tiger Woods, 1997–2002

LPGA Player with the Most
Career Holes in One

Kathy Whitworth

Kathy Whitworth made 11 holes in one during LPGA tournaments in her career. She joined the LPGA in 1958 and was named Player of the Year seven times. She was also named the Associated Press Athlete of the Year twice. Whitworth was the LPGA's leading money winner eight times and was the first female golfer in history to earn $1 million. Along with fellow pro female golfer Mickey Wright, Whitworth made history as one of the first women to compete in the PGA's Legends of Golf. She was inducted into the LPGA Hall of Fame in 1975.

LPGA PLAYERS WITH THE MOST CAREER HOLES IN ONE

Holes in one

Kathy Whitworth, 1958–1990	Vicki Fergon, 1977–	Meg Mallon, 1986–	Jan Stephenson, 1974–	Mickey Wright, 1955–1981
11	8	8	8	8

Country with the Most
World Cup Points

Brazil

COUNTRIES WITH THE
MOST WORLD CUP POINTS

Total points

Brazil, 1958–2002	Germany/ W. Germany, 1954–2002	Italy, 1934–1982	Argentina, 1978–1986	Uruguay, 1930–1950
30	29	21	14	10

Brazil has accumulated 30 points in World Cup championships. (A win is worth four points, runner-up is worth three points, third place is worth two points, and fourth place is worth one point.) In Brazil, soccer is both the national sport and the national pastime. Many Brazilian superstar players are even considered national heroes. The World Cup was organized by the Federation Internationale de Football Association (FIFA) and is played every four years. This international competition was first played in 1930. Both professional and amateur players are allowed to compete.

Man with the Most World Cup Goals

Gerd Müller

rd Müller Str.

Gerd Müller, a striker for West Germany, scored a total of 14 goals in the 1970 and 1974 World Cups. During his impressive soccer career, Müller competed in many other international championships and earned several awards. Müller received the Golden Boot Award (European Top Scorer) in 1970 and 1972, and the European Footballer of the Year Award in 1970. In 1970, he was also the European Championship Top Scorer and was later part of the winning European Championship team in 1972.

MEN WITH THE MOST WORLD CUP GOALS

Goals scored

14	13	12	12	11
Gerd Müller, W. Germany	Just Fontaine, France	Pelé, Brazil	Ronaldo, Brazil	Sandor Kocsis, Hungary

Woman with the Most CAPS

Kristine Lilly

Kristine Lilly holds the world record for the most CAPS, or international games played, with 291. This is the highest number of CAPS in both the men's and women's international soccer organizations. In world standings, she is third in all-time goals scored with 81. In 2004, Lilly scored her 100th international goal, becoming only one of five women to ever accomplish that.

WOMEN WITH THE MOST CAPS

Career CAPS

Kristine Lilly, USA, 1987–	Mia Hamm, USA, 1987–2004	Julie Foudy, USA, 1988–2004	Joy Fawcett, USA, 1987–2004	Brandi Chastain, USA, 1988–2004
291	275	271	239	192

Woman with the Most Pro
Soccer Goals Scored

Mia Hamm

**WOMEN WITH THE MOST PRO
SOCCER GOALS SCORED**

Total career goals

Mia Hamm, USA	Elisabetta Vignotto, Italy	Sun Wen, China	Michelle Akers, USA	Kristine Lilly, USA
158	107	105	105	101

Soccer star Mia Hamm has scored 158 goals in competition during her stellar 18 years in professional soccer. At 15, she began her career as the youngest player ever to compete for the U.S. National Team in 1987. Since then she scored goals in 13 countries against 25 different national teams. Hamm appeared in 274 games in her 18-year career and totaled 142 assists. She also helped the U.S.A. win two World Cup titles and two Olympic gold medals. Hamm retired from the game in 2004.

Most Victories in the
Indianapolis 500

A.J. Foyt, Jr., Rick Mears, and Al Unser

Three of professional car racing's greatest drivers—Rick Mears, A.J. Foyt, Jr., and Al Unser—have each won the Indianapolis 500 a total of four times. Of the three champion drivers, Rick Mears had the fastest time with 2 hours, 50 minutes, and 1 second in 1991. Amazingly, one of Mears's Indy 500 victories was only his second Indy race. The Indianapolis 500 is held on the Indianapolis Motor Speedway. This 2.5-mile-long (4 km) oval track has four turns. The Indy 500 is still considered the most prestigious event in all of professional racing. The race has been held each year since 1911, with the exception of World War I (1917–1918) and World War II (1942–1945).

Al Unser

DRIVERS WHO HAVE THE MOST
INDIANAPOLIS 500 VICTORIES

Number of Indianapolis 500 races won

A.J. Foyt, Jr., 1960–1981	Rick Mears, 1977–1994	Al Unser, 1965–1987	Johnny Rutherford, 1963–1988	Bobby Unser, 1963–1981
4	4	4	3	3

Most Wins in the Daytona 500

Richard Petty

Between 1964 and 1981, Richard Petty won seven Daytona 500 races. He was the first race car driver ever to win the Daytona 500 twice. During his entire 34-year career, he won a total of 200 NASCAR races, including seven Winston Cup championships. Petty was also the first stock-car driver with winnings exceeding $1 million. By the end of his impressive career he had 356 top-5 finishes and was the first driver ever to win 10 consecutive races. His earnings totaled more than $7.7 million. Petty retired from racing in 1992.

DRIVERS WITH THE
MOST DAYTONA 500 WINS

Daytona 500 wins

Driver	Wins
Richard Petty, 1958–1992	7
Bobby Allison, 1966–1988	3
Cale Yarborough, 1965–1985	3
Dale Jarrett, 1984–	3
Michael Waltrip, 2001–	2

Top CART Career
Money Winners

Al Unser, Jr.

During his 18-year Championship Auto Racing Teams (CART) career, Al Unser, Jr. earned an unprecedented $18.8 million. He logged 273 CART starts, winning 31 of the races and accumulating 2,253 points. He was also a CART Champion in 1990 and 1994. He left CART racing in 2000 to drive in Indy Racing League (IRL) IndyCar Series competitions. He is currently part of the Kelley Racing Team and has won three IRL competitions. During his career, Unser has also won the Indianapolis 500, the Daytona 500, and the International Race of Champions (IROC) two times each.

TOP CART CAREER
MONEY WINNERS

Career winnings
in millions of US dollars

Al Unser, Jr., 1982–1999	Michael Andretti, 1983–2002	Bobby Rahal, 1982–1998	Emerson Fittipaldi, 1984–1996	Mario Andretti, 1979–1994
$18.8 M	$17.9 M	$16.3 M	$14.3 M	$11.6 M

Country with the Most
Tour de France Wins

France

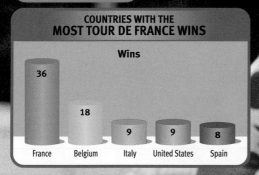

**COUNTRIES WITH THE
MOST TOUR DE FRANCE WINS**

Wins

France	Belgium	Italy	United States	Spain
36	18	9	9	8

French cyclists have won the prestigious Tour de France a record 36 times. This is not surprising because competitive cycling is a very popular pastime in the country. Two of France's most successful riders—Jacques Anquetil and Bernard Hinault—have each won the race five times. Held each July, the Tour de France lasts from 25 to 30 days. Approximately 150 cyclists compete in teams and race through about 2,000 miles (3,220 km) of France's landscape. Occasionally, the course may also extend through parts of Belgium, Spain, Germany, and Switzerland.

Bernard Hinault

117

Fastest Man in the Olympic
100 Meters

Donovan Bailey

Canadian sprinter Donovan Bailey set an Olympic record at the 1996 Atlanta Games when he completed the 100 meters (328 ft) in 9.84 seconds. That means Donovan was running at a speed of about 22.7 miles (36.5 km) per hour. He also took home a gold medal in the 4 X 100 meter event. Donovan became the first of only two men ever to hold all three titles of Olympic Champion, World Champion, and World Record Holder at the same time. A native of Jamaica, he also holds four World Championship medals and one Commonwealth medal.

FASTEST MEN IN THE OLYMPIC
100 METERS

Time in seconds

9.84	9.85	9.87	9.92	9.96
Donovan Bailey, Canada, 1996	Justin Gatlin, USA, 2004	Maurice Greene, USA, 2004	Carl Lewis, USA, 1988	Linford Christie, Great Britain, 1992

Fastest Woman in the Olympic
100 Meters

Florence Griffith-Joyner

Florence Griffith-Joyner—also known as Flo Jo—sprinted the 100 meters (328 ft) at the 1988 Seoul Olympic Games in just 10.54 seconds. She also won a gold medal for the 200-meter (656-ft) dash and the 400-meter (1312-ft) relay that year. Flo Jo also holds the world records for both the 100- and 200-meter dashes, and is one of only two women to ever run the 200 meters (656 ft) in under 21.70 seconds. For all of her impressive achievements, she was named the Associated Press Athlete of the Year, U.S. Olympic Committee Sportswoman of the Year, and Jesse Owens Outstanding Track and Field Athlete in 1988. Flo Jo passed away in 1998.

FASTEST WOMEN IN THE OLYMPIC 100 METERS

Time in seconds

10.54	10.75	10.82	10.93	10.94
Florence Griffith-Joyner, USA, 1988	Marion Jones, USA, 2000	Gail Devers, USA, 1992	Yuliya Nesterenko, Belarus, 2004	Gail Devers, USA, 1992

Athletes with the Most Medals in One Olympics

Aleksandr Dityatin/ Michael Phelps

Aleksandr Dityatin and Michael Phelps each won a total of eight medals in one Olympics. Dityatin was a Soviet gymnast in the 1980 Olympics in Moscow, Soviet Union. Competing in front of the hometown crowd, he took gold in the team competition and the individual all-around. Dityatin then won six medals in one day: one gold, four silvers, and one bronze. In the 2004 Olympics in Athens, Greece, Phelps swam his way to six gold medals and two bronze. He was the first American male to qualify for six individual events. Phelps holds three Olympic records.

ATHLETES WITH THE MOST MEDALS IN ONE OLYMPICS

Medals won

Aleksandr Dityatin, USSR, 1980	Michael Phelps, USA, 2004	Nikolai Andrianov, USSR, 1976	Matt Biondi, USA, 1988	Mark Spitz, USA, 1972
8	8	7	7	7

World's Fastest Olympic
Bobsled Time

Germany II

WORLD'S FASTEST OLYMPIC
BOBSLED TIMES

Time (minutes:seconds)

Germany II, 1998	Germany II, 2002	East Germany, 1984	Germany, 1994	East Germany, 1976
2:39.41	3:07.51	3:20.22	3:27.28	3:40.43

At the 1998 Winter Olympics in Nagano, Japan, Germany II sped down the bobsled track and into the history books with a record-breaking time of 2:39.41. The team of four men—Christoph Langen, Markus Zimmermann, Marco Jakobs, and Olaf Hampel—followed the German tradition of excellence in bobsledding. In fact, the five fastest bobsled times were all accomplished by Germans. A bobsled can reach a speed of 90 miles (145 km) per hour, and the crew feels five times the force of gravity when braking. The sport became an Olympic competition in 1924.

Fastest Man in Olympic Downhill Skiing

Fritz Strobl

During the 2002 Olympics in Salt Lake City, Utah, Austrian skier Fritz Strobl flew down the course and grabbed the gold with a time of 1:39.13. The 1.9-mile (3.1-km) course—nicknamed The Grizzly—was said to be one of the toughest in Olympic competition. It was shorter than most other courses, but it included a vertical drop of 3,000 feet (914 m) and wound through the Wasatch-Cache National Forest. Strobl, a 29-year-old policeman from Lienz, also won two other major competitions the same year—Bormio and Garmisch-Partenkirchen.

FASTEST MEN IN OLYMPIC DOWNHILL SKIING

Time (minutes:seconds)

Fritz Strobl, Austria, 2002	Bill Johnson, USA, 1984	Leonhard Stock, Austria, 1980	Franz Klammer, Austria, 1976	Tommy Moe, USA, 1994
1:39.13	1:45.49	1:45.50	1:45.73	1:45.75

Fastest Woman in Olympic
Downhill Skiing

Michela Figini

Skiing sensation Michela Figini of Switzerland won the downhill skiing gold medal at the 1984 Olympic Games in Sarajevo, Yugoslavia, with a time of 1:13.36. At the age of 17, Figini became the youngest Olympian to earn a medal in Alpine skiing. She became known for her strict self-discipline during training and her graceful moves on the course. Figini is a native of southern Ticino, Switzerland, and speaks fluent Italian.

**FASTEST WOMEN IN OLYMPIC
DOWNHILL SKIING**

Time (minutes:seconds)

Michela Figini, Switzerland, 1984	Marina Kiehl, W. Germany, 1988	Katja Seizinger, Germany, 1998	Katja Seizinger, Germany, 1994	Marie-Thérèse Nadig, Switzerland, 1972
1:13.36	1:25.86	1:28.89	1:35.93	1:36.68

Fastest Man in Olympic 500 Meters
Speed Skating

American speed skater Casey FitzRandolph won gold in the 500 meter (1,640 ft) short track at the 2002 Salt Lake City, Utah, Olympics with a time of 34.42. This means that he averaged 14.5 meters (47.6 ft) per second! During this event, competitors have two separate opportunities to race on the same day, and the times are averaged together to determine the winner. FitzRandolph has also medaled in the United States and World Championships.

Casey FitzRandolph

FASTEST MEN IN OLYMPIC 500 METERS
SPEED SKATING

Time (minutes:seconds)

Casey FitzRandolph, USA, 2002	Hiroyasu Shimizu, Japan, 1998	Aleksander Golubev, Russia, 1994	Uwe-Jens May, E. Germany, 1988	Uwe-Jens May, Germany, 1992
0:34.42	0:35.59	0:36.33	0:36.45	0:37.14

Fastest Woman in Olympic 500 Meters
Speed Skating

Catriona Le May Doan

FASTEST WOMEN IN OLYMPIC 500 METERS
SPEED SKATING

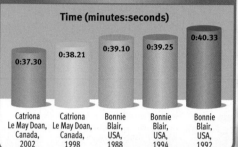

Time (minutes:seconds)

Time	Skater
0:37.30	Catriona Le May Doan, Canada, 2002
0:38.21	Catriona Le May Doan, Canada, 1998
0:39.10	Bonnie Blair, USA, 1988
0:39.25	Bonnie Blair, USA, 1994
0:40.33	Bonnie Blair, USA, 1992

Catriona Le May Doan has earned the title as the Fastest Woman on Ice. At the 2002 Olympics in Salt Lake City, Utah, the speed skater completed the 500-meter (1,640-ft) track in just 37.30 seconds—beating her own record from the previous Olympics. In doing this, she became the first Canadian to defend her gold in an individual Olympic competition. She also holds the world record in this event. Le May Doan is a three-time recipient of the Canadian Female Athlete of the Year award.

Most Career Points

Wayne Gretzky

During his 20-year career, Wayne Gretzky scored an unbelievable 2,857 points and 894 goals. In fact, Gretzky was the first person in the NHL to average more than two points per game. Many people consider Canadian-born Gretzky to be the greatest player in the history of the National Hockey League. In fact, he is called the "Great One." He officially retired from the sport in 1999 and was inducted into the Hockey Hall of Fame that same year. After his final game, the NHL retired his jersey number (99).

PLAYERS WHO SCORED THE MOST CAREER POINTS

Points scored

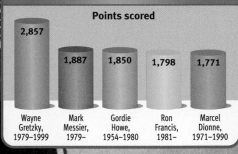

Wayne Gretzky, 1979–1999	Mark Messier, 1979–	Gordie Howe, 1954–1980	Ron Francis, 1981–	Marcel Dionne, 1971–1990
2,857	1,887	1,850	1,798	1,771

Team with the Most
Stanley Cup Wins

Montreal Canadiens

Between 1916 and 1993, the Montreal Canadiens have won an amazing 24 Stanley Cup victories. That's almost one-quarter of all the Stanley Cups ever played. The team plays at Montreal's Molson Center. The Canadiens were created in December 1909 by J. Ambrose O'Brien to play for the National Hockey Association (NHA). They eventually made the transition into the National Hockey League. Over the years, the Canadiens have included such great players as Maurice Richard, George Hainsworth, Jacques Lemaire, Saku Koivu, and Emile Bouchard.

TEAMS WITH THE MOST STANLEY CUP WINS

Stanley Cups won

24	11	10	5	5
Montreal Canadiens, 1916–1993	Toronto Maple Leafs, 1932–1967	Detroit Red Wings, 1936–2002	Boston Bruins, 1929–1972	Edmonton Oilers, 1984–1990

Montreal Canadiens with Stanley Cup

Most Points in a Single Game

Darryl Sittler

PLAYERS WITH THE MOST POINTS EARNED IN A SINGLE GAME

Points

Darryl Sittler, 1976	Tom Bladon, 1977	Bert Olmstead, 1954	Maurice Richard, 1944	Bryan Trotier, 1978
10	8	8	8	8

Toronto Maple Leaf Darryl Sittler scored 6 goals and had 4 assists to earn a record total of 10 points in a game against the Boston Bruins on February 7, 1976. In an added dramatic flourish, the last goal he scored was actually from behind the net. Sittler tried to pass to a teammate, but the puck bounced off another player's leg and into the net instead. Sittler played professionally for 15 seasons in the National Hockey League and was inducted into the Hockey Hall of Fame in 1989.

Goalie with the
Most Career Wins

Patrick Roy

Patrick Roy won 551 games during his impressive hockey career. Roy also holds the NHL records for most 30-or-more win seasons (11), most playoff games played (240), most playoff minutes played (14,783), and most playoff wins (148). He was also a member of the Montreal Canadiens when they won the Stanley Cup in 1986 and 1993. Roy helped his team—the Colorado Avalanche—to win the Stanley Cup Championships in 1996 and 2001. On May 29, 2003, Roy announced his retirement from the sport.

**GOALTENDERS WITH THE
MOST CAREER WINS**

Games won

551	447	434	423	407
Patrick Roy, 1984–2003	Terry Sawchuck, 1945–1970	Jacques Plante, 1951–1975	Tony Esposito, 1963–1981	Glenn Hall, 1952–1971

Nature Records

Animals • Disasters • Food
Natural Formations • Plants • Weather

World's Sleepiest Animal

Koala

A koala will spend the majority of its day—about 22 hours—sleeping in its eucalyptus tree. Its sharp claws and nimble feet help it to hold on to the branches, even when it is asleep. Koalas are nocturnal animals, which means they are active mainly at night. During the 2 hours a koala is awake, it will feed on 1 to 2 pounds (.4 to .9 kg) of eucalyptus leaves. When a koala is born, it measures about 3/4 inch (1.9 cm) long and lives in its mother's pouch for six months. An average koala is about 2 feet (.6 m) tall and weighs about 22 pounds (10 kg).

THE WORLD'S SLEEPIEST ANIMALS

Hours of sleep per day

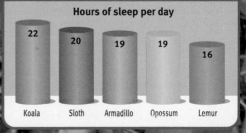

Koala	Sloth	Armadillo	Opossum	Lemur
22	20	19	19	16

World's Fastest Land Mammal

Cheetah

These sleek mammals can reach a speed of 65 miles (105 km) per hour for short spurts. Their quickness enables these large African cats to easily outrun their prey. All other African cats must stalk their prey because they lack the cheetah's amazing speed. Unlike the paws of all other cats, cheetah paws do not have skin sheaths—thin protective coverings. Their claws, therefore, cannot pull back.

THE WORLD'S FASTEST LAND MAMMALS

Maximum speed in miles/kilometers per hour

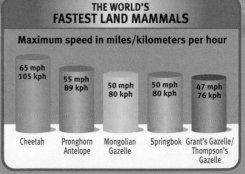

Cheetah	Pronghorn Antelope	Mongolian Gazelle	Springbok	Grant's Gazelle/ Thompson's Gazelle
65 mph 105 kph	55 mph 89 kph	50 mph 80 kph	50 mph 80 kph	47 mph 76 kph

World's
Slowest Land Mammal

Sloth

When a three-toed sloth is traveling on the ground, it reaches a top speed of only .07 miles (.11 km) per hour. That means that it would take the animal almost 15 minutes to cross a four-lane street. The main reason sloths move so slowly is that they cannot walk like other mammals. They must pull themselves along the ground using only their sharp claws. Because of this, sloths spend the majority of their time in trees. A green algae grows on their fur, camouflaging them in the trees. Surprisingly, sloths are distantly related to armadillos and anteaters.

SOME OF THE WORLD'S SLOWEST LAND MAMMALS

Maximum speed in miles/kilometers per hour

Sloth	Guinea Pig	Mouse	Pig	Squirrel
.07 mph .11 kph	5 mph 8.1 kph	8 mph 12.9 kph	11 mph 18 kph	12 mph 19 kph

133

World's
Smallest Mammal

Kitti's Hog-nosed Bat

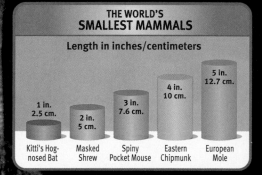

**THE WORLD'S
SMALLEST MAMMALS**

Length in inches/centimeters

Kitti's Hog-nosed Bat	Masked Shrew	Spiny Pocket Mouse	Eastern Chipmunk	European Mole
1 in. 2.5 cm.	2 in. 5 cm.	3 in. 7.6 cm.	4 in. 10 cm.	5 in. 12.7 cm.

The Kitti's hog-nosed bat weighs a mere .25 ounce (7.1 g) and measures about 1 inch (2.5 cm) wide. This means that the world's smallest mammal is actually the size of a bumblebee. Even when its wings are extended, this member of the bat family measures only 6 inches (15 cm) wide. This tiny creature is found only in Thailand. It lives in the limestone caves near the Kwae Noi River. Like most bats, Kitti's hog-nosed bats are most active from dusk until dawn and feed mostly on insects.

World's Tallest
Land Mammal

Giraffe

Giraffes can grow to more than 18 feet (5.5 m) in height. That means an average giraffe could look through the window of a two-story building. A giraffe's neck is 18 times longer than a human's, but both mammals have exactly the same number of neck bones. A giraffe's long legs enable it to outrun most of its enemies. When cornered, a giraffe has been known to kill a lion with a single kick.

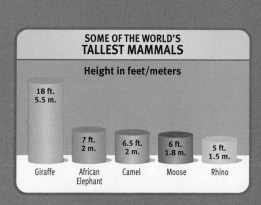

SOME OF THE WORLD'S TALLEST MAMMALS

Height in feet/meters

18 ft. 5.5 m.	7 ft. 2 m.	6.5 ft. 2 m.	6 ft. 1.8 m.	5 ft. 1.5 m.
Giraffe	African Elephant	Camel	Moose	Rhino

World's Heaviest
Marine Mammal

Blue Whale

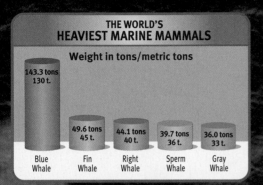

THE WORLD'S HEAVIEST MARINE MAMMALS

Weight in tons/metric tons

143.3 tons 130 t.	49.6 tons 45 t.	44.1 tons 40 t.	39.7 tons 36 t.	36.0 tons 33 t.
Blue Whale	Fin Whale	Right Whale	Sperm Whale	Gray Whale

Blue whales can weigh more than 143 tons (130 t) and measure over 100 feet (30 m) long, making these enormous sea creatures the largest animals that have ever lived. Amazingly, these gentle giants only eat krill—small, shrimplike animals. A blue whale can eat about 4 tons (3.6 t) of krill each day in the summer, when food is plentiful . To catch the krill, a whale gulps as much as 17,000 gallons (64,600 l) of seawater into its mouth at one time. Then it uses its tongue—which can be the same size as a car—to push the water back out. The krill get caught in hairs on the whale's baleen (a keratin structure that hangs down from the roof of the whale's mouth).

World's Heaviest
Land Mammal

African Elephant

African elephants measure approximately 24 feet (7.3 m) long and can weigh up to 6 tons (5.4 t). Even at their great size, they are strictly vegetarian. They will, however, eat up to 500 pounds (226 kg) of vegetation a day! Their two tusks—which are really elongated teeth—grow continuously during their lives and can reach about 9 feet (2.7 m) in length. These large animals move at about 4 miles (6.4 km) per hour, but they can charge at 30 miles (48 km) per hour.

THE WORLD'S HEAVIEST LAND MAMMALS

In pounds/kilograms

African Elephant	White Rhinoceros	Hippopotamus	Giraffe	American Bison
14,432 lb. 6,546 kg.	7,937 lb. 3,600 kg.	5,512 lb. 2,300 kg.	3,527 lb. 1,600 kg.	2,205 lb. 1,000 kg.

137

World's
Largest Rodent

Capybara

Also known as water hogs and carpinchos, capybaras reach an average length of 4 feet (1.2 m), stand about 20 inches (51 cm) tall, and weigh between 75 and 150 pounds (34 to 68 kg)! That's about the same size as a Labrador retriever. Capybaras are found in South and Central America, where they spend much of their time in groups looking for food. They are strictly vegetarian and have been known to raid gardens for melons and squash. Their partially webbed feet make capybaras excellent swimmers. Capybaras are hunted for food and their hides are used for gloves and clothing.

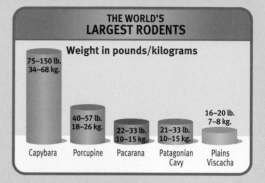

THE WORLD'S LARGEST RODENTS

Weight in pounds/kilograms

- Capybara: 75–150 lb. / 34–68 kg.
- Porcupine: 40–57 lb. / 18–26 kg.
- Pacarana: 22–33 lb. / 10–15 kg.
- Patagonian Cavy: 21–33 lb. / 10–15 kg.
- Plains Viscacha: 16–20 lb. / 7–8 kg.

World's Longest-Lived
Mammal

Killer Whale

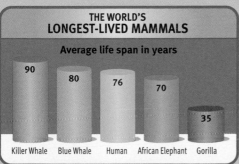

THE WORLD'S
LONGEST-LIVED MAMMALS

Average life span in years

Killer Whale	Blue Whale	Human	African Elephant	Gorilla
90	80	76	70	35

The average life span of a killer whale is 90 years. The average life span of a human is only about 76 years. Male killer whales can measure up to 28 feet (9m) long and weigh up to 12,000 pounds (5,443 kg). They have more than 4 dozen razor-sharp teeth and use them to feed on both birds and mammals. Some of these whales have been known to eat up to 2,000 pounds (907 kg) in just one feeding.

World's Fastest Flyer

Peregrine Falcon

When diving through the air, a peregrine falcon can reach speeds of up to 175 miles (282 km) an hour. That's about the same speed as the fastest race car in the Indianapolis 500. These powerful birds can catch prey in midair and kill it instantly with their sharp claws. Peregrine falcons range from about 13 to 19 inches (33 to 48 cm) long. The female is called a falcon, but the male is called a tercel, which means "one-third" in German. This is because the male is about one-third the size of the female.

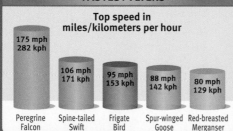

THE WORLD'S FASTEST FLYERS

Top speed in miles/kilometers per hour

Peregrine Falcon	Spine-tailed Swift	Frigate Bird	Spur-winged Goose	Red-breasted Merganser
175 mph 282 kph	106 mph 171 kph	95 mph 153 kph	88 mph 142 kph	80 mph 129 kph

World's Largest Bird Wingspan

Marabou Stork

The Marabou stork has the largest wingspan of any bird. With a wingspan that can reach up to 13 feet (4 m), these large storks weigh up to 20 pounds (9 kg) and can grow up to 5 feet (150 cm) tall. Their long leg and toe bones are actually hollow. This adaptation is very important for flight because it makes the bird lighter. Although marabous eat insects, small mammals, and fish, the majority of their food is carrion—already dead meat. Since these storks need to eat about 1.5 pounds (700 g) of food a day, this makes them an important part of nature's clean-up crew.

THE WORLD'S LARGEST BIRD WINGSPANS

Wingspan in feet/meters

Marabou Stork	Albatross	Trumpeter Swan	Mute Swan	Whooper Swan
13 ft. 4 m.	12 ft. 3.7 m.	11 ft. 3.4 m.	10 ft. 3 m.	10 ft. 3 m

141

Bird That Builds the Largest Nest

Bald Eagle

A bald eagle's nest can measure 8 feet (2.4 m) wide and 16 feet (4.9 m) deep. These birds of prey have wingspans up to 7.5 feet (2.3m) and need a home that they can nest in comfortably. By carefully constructing their home with sticks, branches, and plant material, a pair of bald eagles can balance their home—which can weigh up to 4,000 pounds (8,800 kg)—on the top of a tree or cliff. Called an aerie, this home will be used for the rest of the eagles' lives. Each year a bald eagle pair will add on to their nest as they prepare to raise more offspring.

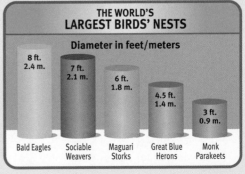

THE WORLD'S LARGEST BIRDS' NESTS

Diameter in feet/meters

Bald Eagles	Sociable Weavers	Maguari Storks	Great Blue Herons	Monk Parakeets
8 ft. 2.4 m.	7 ft. 2.1 m.	6 ft. 1.8 m.	4.5 ft. 1.4 m.	3 ft. 0.9 m.

World's Largest
Flightless Bird

Ostrich

An ostrich can grow up to 8 feet (2.4 m) tall and weigh up to 300 pounds (136 kg). Ostriches also have the largest eyeballs of the bird class, measuring 2 inches (5 cm) across. These African birds lay giant eggs, averaging 3 pounds (1.4 kg) each. Ostriches can run at speeds of up to 50 miles (80.5 km) per hour. With their long legs, they can cover 15 feet (4.6 m) in a single bound. Ostriches live on the hot, grassy plains of Africa and eat plants, insects, seeds, and fruits.

THE WORLD'S LARGEST FLIGHTLESS BIRDS

Height in inches/centimeters

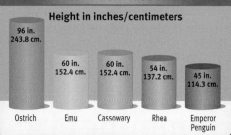

96 in. 243.8 cm.	60 in. 152.4 cm.	60 in. 152.4 cm.	54 in. 137.2 cm.	45 in. 114.3 cm.
Ostrich	Emu	Cassowary	Rhea	Emperor Penguin

World's Smallest Bird

From the tip of its bill to the end of its tail, the male bee hummingbird measures barely 2.5 inches (6.3 cm) long. In fact, its tail and bill alone make up one-half of the bird's length, which is about equal to the width of a baseball card. Bee hummingbirds, which weigh only about .07 ounce (2 g), are also able to beat their wings at speeds of up to 80 times per second. Like most other hummingbirds, they are able to fly forward, backward, and straight up and down. They also have the unique ability to hover in midair. These tiny flying creatures are found in Cuba and on the Isle of Pines in the South Pacific.

THE WORLD'S SMALLEST BIRDS

Length in inches/centimeters

Bird	Length
Bee Hummingbird	2.5 in. 6.3 cm.
Pygmy Parrot	3.5 in. 9.0 cm.
New Zealand Wren	3.5 in. 9.0 cm.
Gouldian Finch	4.0 in. 10.0 cm.
Least Sandpiper	4.5 in. 11.0 cm.

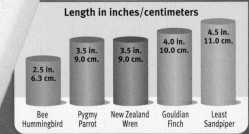

Bee Hummingbird

World's Largest Bird Egg

Ostrich Egg

An ostrich egg can measure 5 inches by 6 inches (13 cm by 16 cm) long and weigh up to 4 pounds (1.8 kg). In fact, just one ostrich egg equals up to 24 chicken eggs. The egg yolk makes up one-third of the volume. Although the egg shell is only 2 mm thick, it is tough enough to withstand the weight of a 345-pound (157-kg) ostrich. A hen ostrich can lay from 10 to 70 eggs each year. Females usually are able to recognize their own eggs, even when they are mixed in with those of other females in their shared nest.

THE WORLD'S LARGEST BIRD EGGS

Weight of egg in pounds/kilograms

Ostrich	Emu	Kiwi	Emperor Penguin	Albatross
4.0 lb. 1.8 kg.	1.8 lb. 0.82 kg.	1.6 lb. 0.72 kg.	1.5 lb. 0.68 kg.	1.0 lb. 0.45 kg.

Creature with the
Most Legs

Illacme Plenipes

Illacme plenipes—a species of millipede found in California—has 750 legs, making it the most-legged creature in the world. Even though the name millipede actually means "thousand legs," most species have fewer than 300 legs. All millipedes have two pairs of legs per body segment that move together, meaning that the first pair of legs can be doing something different than a pair three rows back. Although millipedes have only a few segments at birth, they add several segments each time they molt—or shed. A mature millipede averages about 50 segments, or 100 legs.

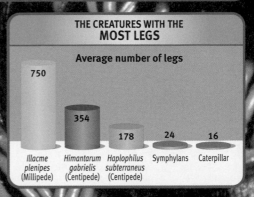

THE CREATURES WITH THE MOST LEGS

Average number of legs

750	354	178	24	16
Illacme plenipes (Millipede)	*Himantarum gabrielis* (Centipede)	*Haplophilus subterraneus* (Centipede)	Symphylans	Caterpillar

World's
Largest Spider

Goliath Birdeater

A Goliath birdeater can grow to a total length of 11 inches (28 cm) and weigh about 6 ounces (170 g). A Goliath's spiderlings are also big—they can have a 6-inch (15-cm) leg span after just one year. These giant tarantulas are found mostly in the rain forests of Guyana, Suriname, Brazil, and Venezuela. The Goliath birdeater's name is misleading—they commonly eat insects and small reptiles. Similar to other tarantula species, the Goliath birdeater lives in a burrow. The spider will wait by the opening to ambush prey that gets too close.

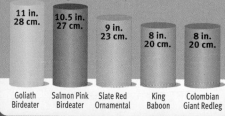

THE WORLD'S LARGEST SPIDERS

Length in inches/centimeters

Goliath Birdeater	Salmon Pink Birdeater	Slate Red Ornamental	King Baboon	Colombian Giant Redleg
11 in. 28 cm.	10.5 in. 27 cm.	9 in. 23 cm.	8 in. 20 cm.	8 in. 20 cm.

World's Fastest Flying Insect

Hawk Moth

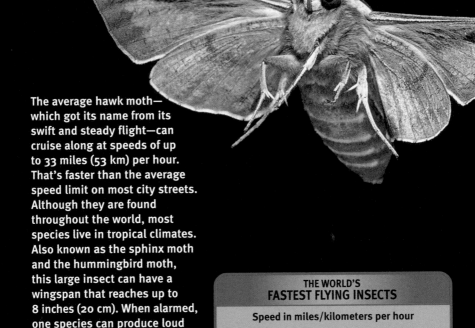

The average hawk moth—which got its name from its swift and steady flight—can cruise along at speeds of up to 33 miles (53 km) per hour. That's faster than the average speed limit on most city streets. Although they are found throughout the world, most species live in tropical climates. Also known as the sphinx moth and the hummingbird moth, this large insect can have a wingspan that reaches up to 8 inches (20 cm). When alarmed, one species can produce loud squawking noises by blowing air through its tongue.

THE WORLD'S FASTEST FLYING INSECTS

Speed in miles/kilometers per hour

Hawk Moth	West Indian Butterfly	Deer Bot Fly	Dragonfly	Hornet
33.3 mph 53.6 kph	30.0 mph 48.2 kph	30.0 mph 48.2 kph	17.8 mph 28.6 kph	13.3 mph 21.4 kph

World's Longest Insect

Stick Insect

THE WORLD'S LONGEST INSECTS

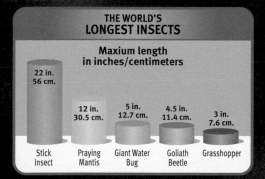

Maxium length in inches/centimeters

Stick Insect	Praying Mantis	Giant Water Bug	Goliath Beetle	Grasshopper
22 in. 56 cm.	12 in. 30.5 cm.	5 in. 12.7 cm.	4.5 in. 11.4 cm.	3 in. 7.6 cm.

Measuring more than 22 inches (56 cm) in length, the tropical stick insect is almost the same size as an average television screen. All together, there are about 2,000 species of stick insects. They feed on plants and are mostly nocturnal. Most have long, thin brown or green bodies. Their twiglike appearance camouflages them well. When they are still, stick insects look just like part of a plant or tree. Their eggs are also camouflaged and look like tiny, hard seeds. All stick insects have the ability to grow back a leg or antenna that has broken off.

149

World's Smallest Fish

Dwarf Pygmy Goby

The dwarf pygmy goby is the world's smallest fish, measuring only .5 inch (13 mm) long at the most. It is also one of the smallest living animals with a backbone. Unlike most gobies, this species lives in freshwater and can be found mainly in the Philippines. These fish must, however, swim to saltwater to breed and hatch their eggs. Gobies usually lay only a few eggs at a time and sometimes care briefly for their young, which are called ipon.

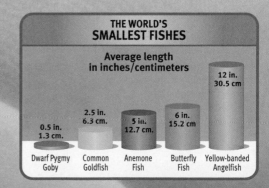

THE WORLD'S SMALLEST FISHES

Average length in inches/centimeters

Dwarf Pygmy Goby	Common Goldfish	Anemone Fish	Butterfly Fish	Yellow-banded Angelfish
0.5 in. 1.3 cm.	2.5 in. 6.3 cm.	5 in. 12.7 cm.	6 in. 15.2 cm	12 in. 30.5 cm

World's
Biggest Fish

Whale Shark

THE WORLD'S BIGGEST FISHES

Average weight in pounds/kilograms

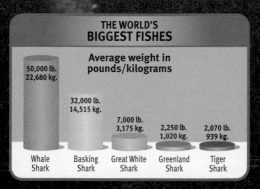

Whale Shark	Basking Shark	Great White Shark	Greenland Shark	Tiger Shark
50,000 lb. 22,680 kg.	32,000 lb. 14,515 kg.	7,000 lb. 3,175 kg.	2,250 lb. 1,020 kg.	2,070 lb. 939 kg.

Whale sharks grow to an average of 30 feet (9 m) in length, but many have been known to reach up to 60 feet (18 m) long. That's the same length as two school buses! Whale sharks also weigh an average of 50,000 pounds (22,680 kg). As with most sharks, the females are larger than the males. Their mouths measure about 5 feet (1.5 m) long and contain about 3,000 teeth. Amazingly, these gigantic fish eat only microscopic plankton and tiny fish. They float near the surface looking for food.

151

World's Fastest Fish

Sailfish

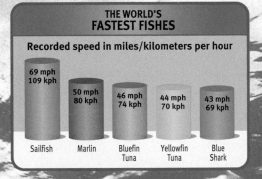

THE WORLD'S FASTEST FISHES

Recorded speed in miles/kilometers per hour

Sailfish	Marlin	Bluefin Tuna	Yellowfin Tuna	Blue Shark
69 mph 109 kph	50 mph 80 kph	46 mph 74 kph	44 mph 70 kph	43 mph 69 kph

Although it is difficult to measure the exact speed of fish, a sailfish once grabbed a fishing line and dragged it 300 feet (91 m) away in just 3 seconds. That means it was swimming at an average speed of 69 miles (109 km) per hour—just higher than the average speed limit on the highway! Sailfish are very large—they average 6 feet (1.8 m) long, but can grow up to 11 feet (3.4 m). Sailfish eat squid and surface-dwelling fish. Sometimes several sailfish will work together to catch their prey.

World's
Slowest Fish

Sea Horse

Sea horses move around the ocean at just .001 miles (.002 km) per hour. At that rate of speed, it would take the fish about an hour to swim only 5 feet (1.5 m). Sea horses spend most of their time near the shore. There, they can hold on to plants with their tails. This helps them avoid enemies. Approximately 50 different species of sea horses are found throughout the world. However, due to over-harvesting, the sea horse population has decreased by up to 95%. Poachers catch sea horses to stock aquariums and also to use as medicines in some countries.

SOME OF THE WORLD'S SLOWEST FISHES

Average speed in miles/kilometers

Sea Horse	Barracuda	Tiger Shark	Tarpon	Swordfish
.001 mph .002 kph	25 mph 40 kph	33 mph 53 kph	35 mph 56 kph	40 mph 64 kph

World's
Largest Mollusk

Giant Squid

THE WORLD'S
LARGEST MOLLUSKS

Length in inches/centimeters

Giant Squid	Giant Clam	Australian Trumpet	Hexabranchus sanguineus	Carinaria cristata
720 in. 1676 cm.	51 in. 130 cm.	30 in. 77 cm.	20 in. 52 cm.	19 in. 50 cm.

The giant squid measures at least 60 feet long (18 m), with tentacles as long as 40 feet (12.2 m) and eyes the size of hubcaps. This giant sea creature may have even more impressive measurements, but scientists have had a very difficult time studying this elusive creature. Living at depths of up to 1,970 feet (600 m) below sea level, scientists have only been able to study dead giant squid that have been caught in fishing nets or eaten by sperm whales. Fewer than 50 giant squid have been found in the last century. As underwater technology advances, scientists hope to be able to study this giant mollusk in greater detail.

Snake with the
Longest Fangs

Gaboon Viper

The Gaboon viper has fangs that measure 2 inches (5 cm) in length! These giant fangs fold up against the snake's mouth so it does not pierce its own skin. When it is ready to strike its prey, the fangs snap down into position. The snake can grow up to 7 feet (2 m) long and weigh 18 pounds (8 kg). It is found in Africa and is perfectly camouflaged for hunting on the ground beneath leaves and grasses. The Gaboon viper's poison is not as toxic as some other snakes, but it is quite dangerous because of the amount of poison it can inject at one time. The snake is not very aggressive, however, and usually only attacks when bothered.

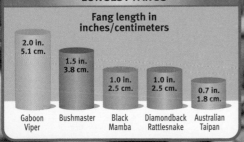

SNAKES WITH THE LONGEST FANGS

Fang length in inches/centimeters

2.0 in. 5.1 cm.	1.5 in. 3.8 cm.	1.0 in. 2.5 cm.	1.0 in. 2.5 cm.	0.7 in. 1.8 cm.
Gaboon Viper	Bushmaster	Black Mamba	Diamondback Rattlesnake	Australian Taipan

World's Deadliest Snake

Black Mamba

One African black mamba snake bite releases a venom powerful enough to kill up to 200 humans. A bite from this snake is almost always fatal if it is not treated immediately. This large member of the cobra family grows to about 14 feet (4.3 m) long. In addition to its deadly poison, it is also a very aggressive snake. It will raise its body off the ground when it feels threatened. It then spreads its hood and strikes swiftly at its prey with its long front teeth. Depending on its age, it can range in color from gray to green to black.

THE WORLD'S DEADLIEST SNAKES

Deaths possible per bite

Black Mamba	Taipan	Russell's Viper	Common Krait	Forest Cobra
200	170	150	60	50

World's Most
Deadly Amphibian

Poison Dart Frog

Poison dart frogs are found mostly in the tropical rain forests of Central and South America, where they live on the moist land. These lethal amphibians have enough poison in their skin to kill up to 20 adult humans. A dart frog's poison is so effective that native Central and South Americans sometimes coat their hunting arrows or hunting darts with it. These brightly colored frogs can be yellow, orange, red, green, blue, or any combination of these colors and measure only .5 to 2 inches (1 to 5 cm) long. They feed mostly on beetles, ants, termites, and other insects by capturing them with their sticky tongues.

SOME OF THE WORLD'S POISONOUS AMPHIBIANS

Length in inches/centimeters

Poison Dart Frog	Black and Yellow Spotted Frog	Fire-bellied Toad	European Salamander	Canetoad
2 in. 5.1 cm.	2.5 in. 6.4 cm.	3 in. 7.6 cm.	4 in. 10 cm.	10 in. 25.4 cm.

World's Longest Snake

Reticulated Python

The average adult reticulated python is about 17 feet (5 m) long, but some can grow to more than 27 feet (8.2 m) in length. That's almost the length of an average school bus. These pythons live mostly in Asia, from Myanmar to Indonesia to the Philippines. The python has teeth that curve backward and can hold the snake's prey still. It hunts mainly at night and will eat mammals and birds. Reticulated pythons are slow-moving creatures that kill their prey by constriction, or strangulation.

THE WORLD'S LONGEST SNAKES

Length in feet/meters

Reticulated Python	Anaconda	Rock Python	King Cobra	Oriental Rat Snake
27.0 ft. 8.2 m.	25.0 ft. 7.6 m.	24.6 ft. 7.5 m.	17.7 ft. 5.4 m.	12.2 ft. 3.7 m.

World's Largest Lizard

Komodo Dragon

These large members of the monitor family can grow to 10 feet (3 m) in length and weigh about 300 pounds (136 kg). A Komodo dragon has a long neck and tail, and strong legs. They are found mainly on Komodo Island. Komodos are dangerous and have even been known to attack and kill humans. A Komodo uses its sense of smell to locate food. It uses its long, yellow tongue to pick up an animal's scent. A Komodo can consume 80% of its body weight in just one meal!

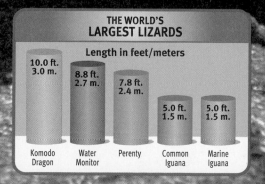

THE WORLD'S LARGEST LIZARDS

Length in feet/meters

Komodo Dragon	Water Monitor	Perenty	Common Iguana	Marine Iguana
10.0 ft. 3.0 m.	8.8 ft. 2.7 m.	7.8 ft. 2.4 m.	5.0 ft. 1.5 m.	5.0 ft. 1.5 m.

World's
Largest Reptile

Saltwater Crocodile

These enormous reptiles can measure more than 22 feet (6.7 m) long. That's about twice the length of the average car. However, males usually measure only about 17 feet (5 m) long, and females normally reach about 10 feet (3 m) in length. A large adult will feed on buffalo, monkeys, cattle, wild boar, and other large mammals. Saltwater crocodiles are found throughout the East Indies and Australia. Despite their name, saltwater crocodiles can also be found in freshwater and swamps. Some other common names for this species are estuarial crocodile and the Indo-Pacific crocodile.

**THE WORLD'S
LARGEST REPTILES**

Maximum length in feet/meters

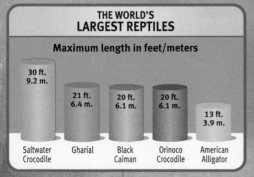

Saltwater Crocodile	Gharial	Black Caiman	Orinoco Crocodile	American Alligator
30 ft. 9.2 m.	21 ft. 6.4 m.	20 ft. 6.1 m.	20 ft. 6.1 m.	13 ft. 3.9 m.

World's
Largest Amphibian

Chinese Giant Salamander

THE WORLD'S LARGEST AMPHIBIANS

Size in inches/centimeters

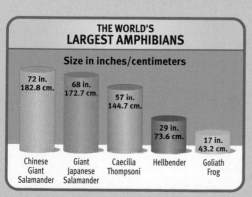

Amphibian	Size
Chinese Giant Salamander	72 in. 182.8 cm.
Giant Japanese Salamander	68 in. 172.7 cm.
Caecilia Thompsoni	57 in. 144.7 cm.
Hellbender	29 in. 73.6 cm.
Goliath Frog	17 in. 43.2 cm.

The Chinese giant salamander can grow to almost 6 feet (1.8 m) in length and weigh up to 55 pounds (25 kg). This amphibian has a large head, but its eyes and nostrils are small. It has short legs, a long tail, and very smooth skin. This large amphibian can be found in the streams of northeastern, central, and southern China. It feeds on fish, frogs, crabs, and snakes. The giant Chinese salamander will not hunt its prey. It will wait until a potential meal wanders too close and then grab it in its mouth. Because many people enjoy the taste of the salamander's meat, it is often hunted and its population is shrinking.

161

World's Longest-Lived
Reptile

Galápagos Tortoise

Some of these giant reptiles have been known to live for more than 150 years. Galápagos tortoises are also some of the largest tortoises in the world, weighing in at up to 500 pounds (226 kg). Even at their great size, these creatures can pull their heads, tails, and legs completely inside their shells. Amazingly, Galápagos tortoises can go without eating or drinking for many weeks. This is partly because it can take them up to three weeks to digest a meal!

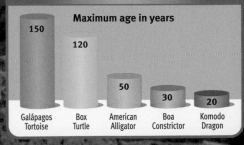

THE WORLD'S LONGEST-LIVED REPTILES

Maximum age in years

Galápagos Tortoise	Box Turtle	American Alligator	Boa Constrictor	Komodo Dragon
150	120	50	30	20

World's Most Destructive
Flood Since 1900

Yangtze River

In August 1998, the raging waters of the Yangtze River spilled over its banks and flooded a 180-mile- (290-km) long stretch of farmland and homes. The high waters remained at dangerous levels for two months in some areas and caused more than 250 million people to evacuate. The total damage from the floods cost more than $30 billion. Approximately 3,000 people lost their lives. The floods were attributed to faulty human-made irrigation, soil erosion, and overdevelopment of the river banks.

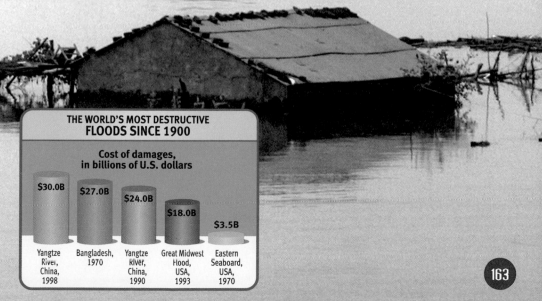

THE WORLD'S MOST DESTRUCTIVE
FLOODS SINCE 1900

Cost of damages,
in billions of U.S. dollars

$30.0B	$27.0B	$24.0B	$18.0B	$3.5B
Yangtze River, China, 1998	Bangladesh, 1970	Yangtze River, China, 1990	Great Midwest Flood, USA, 1993	Eastern Seaboard, USA, 1970

World's Most Intense Earthquake Since 1900

Coastal Chile

On May 22, 1960, the coast of Chile was rocked by an explosive earthquake measuring 9.6 on the Richter scale. This is equal to the intensity of about 60,000 hydrogen bombs. Some 2,000 people were killed and another 3,000 injured. The death toll was fairly low because the foreshocks frightened people into the streets. When the massive jolt came, many of the collapsed buildings were already empty. The coastal towns of Valdivia and Puerto Montt suffered the most damage because they were closest to the epicenter—located about 100 miles (161 km) offshore.

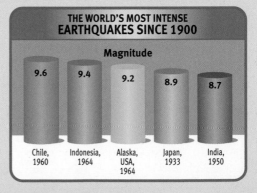

THE WORLD'S MOST INTENSE EARTHQUAKES SINCE 1900

Magnitude

Chile, 1960	Indonesia, 1964	Alaska, USA, 1964	Japan, 1933	India, 1950
9.6	9.4	9.2	8.9	8.7

World's Most Destructive
Tornado Since 1900

Oklahoma City

A devastating tornado swept through downtown Oklahoma City, Oklahoma, on May 3, 1999, killing 36 people and causing more than $1.2 billion in damages. This powerful twister traveled almost 38 miles (61 km) in four hours and measured a mile (1.6 km) wide at times. With raging winds reaching 318 miles (512 km) per hour, it was the strongest wind speed ever recorded. More than 800 houses were destroyed in Oklahoma City alone. Because of the mass destruction caused by this twister, it was classified as a five—the second-highest possible rating—on the Fujita Tornado Scale.

THE WORLD'S MOST DESTRUCTIVE
TORNADOES SINCE 1900

Cost of damages, in millions and billions of U.S. dollars

$1.2B — Oklahoma City, OK, 1999
$1.1B — Omaha, NE, 1975
$1.0B — Missouri, Illinois, Indiana, 1925
$450M — Pennsylvania, Ohio, 1985
$291M — Mid-Atlantic and Ohio Valleys, 1992

165

World's Most Intense
Hurricane Since 1900

Hurricane Gilbert

THE WORLD'S MOST INTENSE
HURRICANES SINCE 1900

Highest sustained wind speed
in miles/kilometers per hour

184 mph 296 kph	180 mph 290 kph	165 mph 266 kph	165 mph 266 kph	140 mph 225 kph
Hurricane Gilbert, 1988	Hurricane Mitch, 1998	Hurricane Allen, 1980	Hurricane Camille, 1969	Florida Keys, 1935

Hurricane Gilbert blew through the Atlantic, Caribbean, and Gulf of Mexico during mid-September 1988, destroying almost everything in its path. It devastated most of the island of Jamaica on September 10th, and later caused major flooding in the Yucatán Peninsula and in Northern Mexico five days later. Gilbert was classified as a category five hurricane—the most destructive hurricane rating on the Saffir-Simpson Hurricane Scale—for five days. The storm's top wind speeds reached 184 miles (296 km) per hour. The total clean-up cost for the hurricane was more than $5 billion. Some 318 people also lost their lives in the terrible storm.

World's Highest
Tsunami Wave Since 1900

Lituya Bay

On July 9, 1958, a tsunami with a wave measuring 1,720 feet (524 m) high crashed down in Lituya Bay, Alaska—an area inside Glacier Bay National Park. The tsunami was caused by a massive landslide that was triggered by an 8.3 magnitude earthquake. The water from the bay covered 5 square miles (13 sq km) of land and traveled inland as far as 3,600 feet (1,097 m). Millions of trees were washed away. Amazingly, because the area was very isolated and the coastline was sheltered by coves, only two people died when their fishing boat sank.

THE WORLD'S HIGHEST
TSUNAMI WAVES SINCE 1900

Height of wave in feet/meters

Lituya Bay, Alaska, USA, 1958	Chile, 1960	The Philippines, 1960	Southern Asia, 2004	Alaska, USA, 1964
1,720 ft. 524 m.	75 ft. 23 m.	60 ft. 18 m.	50 ft. 15 m.	20 ft. 6 m.

Country with the Most Fast-Food Restaurants

There are approximately 555,200 fast-food restaurants in China, and many of them are less than 10 years old. The fast-food craze caught on in China because the restaurants are so much more affordable than many of the other eating places in the country. The most popular fast-food restaurant in China is KFC, followed by McDonald's, California Fried Chicken, and Pizza Hut. Some of the most popular Asian fast-food chains include Japan's Mos Burger and Hong Kong's Café de Coral.

COUNTRIES WITH THE MOST FAST-FOOD RESTAURANTS

Number of restaurants

Country	Number
China	555,200
USA	178,650
India	39,100
Japan	38,592
UK	26,600

World's Largest Fruit

Pumpkin

Although the average size of a pumpkin can vary greatly depending on the variety and species, the greatest weight ever attained by a fruit belongs to a pumpkin. The largest pumpkin ever grown (and recorded) weighed a remarkable 1,061 pounds (481 kg). Pumpkins have a long tradition in the United States and were served at the first Thanksgiving. Today, pumpkins are used mainly in pies, soups, and puddings. People also carve faces in pumpkins on Halloween. In Europe, pumpkin is usually served as a meal's side dish.

THE WORLD'S LARGEST FRUITS

Maximum weight in pounds/kilograms

Fruit	Maximum weight
Pumpkin	1,061 lb. / 481.3 kg.
Watermelon	50 lb. / 22.7 kg.
Banana Squash	32 lb. / 14.5 kg.
Indian Moschata Squash	18 lb. / 8.2 kg.
Casaba Melon	9 lb. / 4.0 kg.

169

World's
Largest Vegetable

Yam

True yams can consistently grow up to 9 feet (2.7 m) long and weigh more than 150 pounds (68 kg). Some specially grown vegetables have been recorded at higher weights than the largest yam, but no other vegetable can consistently reach this size and weight. Even though these giant tropical tuber roots are capable of reaching such a great size, they are usually harvested when they reach about 6 pounds (2.7 kg). While yams are a major food crop in several countries, some varieties are more valuable for the medicinal ingredient they produce.

THE WORLD'S LARGEST VEGETABLES

Maximum weight in pounds/kilograms

Yam	Cabbage	Cauliflower	Turnip	Broccoli
150 lb. 68 kg.	124 lb. 56 kg.	52 lb. 24 kg.	35 lb. 16 kg.	28 lb. 13 kg.

Country That Eats the Most Chocolate

Switzerland

In Switzerland, the average person consumes about 25 pounds (11.4 kg) of chocolate each year. That means approximately 181 million pounds (82 million kg) of chocolate are eaten in this small country annually. Chocolate has always been a popular food around the world. In fact, each year, approximately 594,000 tons (538,758 t) of cocoa beans—an important ingredient in chocolate—are consumed worldwide. Chocolate is consumed mainly in the form of candy, but it is also used to make beverages, to flavor recipes, and to glaze various sweets and bakery products.

THE WORLD'S TOP CHOCOLATE-EATING COUNTRIES

Annual chocolate consumption per capita in pounds/kilograms

Switzerland	UK	Belgium	Germany	Ireland
25.0 lb. 11.4 kg.	20.9 lb. 9.5 kg.	19.1 lb. 8.7 kg.	19.1 lb. 8.7 kg.	17.8 lb. 8.1 kg.

Country That Eats the
Most Meat

United States

Each person in the United States will eat about 268 pounds (122 kg) of meat this year. That's the same weight as 75 phone books. Beef is the most commonly eaten meat in the United States. Each American eats about 63 pounds (29 kg) per year. In fact, an average 45 million pounds (20.4 million kg) of beef are eaten in the United States each day. The most common way to eat beef is in the form of a hamburger or cheeseburger. More than 85% of U.S. citizens ate one of these fast food items last year. Chicken is the second most popular meat, with each American eating about 62 pounds (28.1 kg) per year.

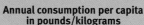

THE COUNTRIES WITH THE HIGHEST MEAT CONSUMPTION

Annual consumption per capita in pounds/kilograms

USA	Spain	Denmark	Australia	Austria
268 lb. 122 kg.	260 lb. 118 kg.	257 lb. 117 kg.	243 lb. 110 kg.	243 lb. 110 kg.

Country That Drinks the Most Tea

Iraq

The people of Iraq each drink about 1,219 cups of tea each year. That means that the middle-eastern country goes through more than 30.86 billion cups a year! Tea is brewed very strong and often served with sweetener. Much of the tea consumed in Iraq is imported, with more than 60% coming from India. Teahouses are very common throughout Iraq and are a popular gathering spot.

THE WORLD'S TOP TEA-DRINKING COUNTRIES

Annual per capita consumption in cups

Iraq	Ireland	Libya	Qatar	UK
1,219	1,214	1,148	1,008	994

Country That Eats the Most Potato Chips

United Kingdom

People in the United Kingdom eat a lot of chips—averaging about 6.4 pounds (2.9 kg) per capita each year. This means that each person snacks on almost 14 bags in just 12 months, and some 8,500 million packages are sold each year! Better known as "crisps" in the United Kingdom, potato chips were first served in 1853 at a lodge in Saratoga Springs, New York. It takes about 10,000 pounds (4,536 kg) of potatoes to make 3,500 pounds (1,588 kg) of chips.

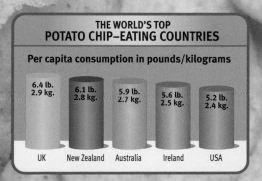

THE WORLD'S TOP POTATO CHIP–EATING COUNTRIES

Per capita consumption in pounds/kilograms

6.4 lb. 2.9 kg.	6.1 lb. 2.8 kg.	5.9 lb. 2.7 kg.	5.6 lb. 2.5 kg.	5.2 lb. 2.4 kg.
UK	New Zealand	Australia	Ireland	USA

Country That Eats the Most Ice Cream

Australia

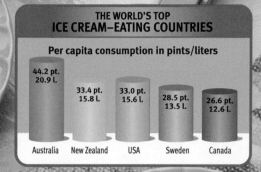

THE WORLD'S TOP ICE CREAM–EATING COUNTRIES

Per capita consumption in pints/liters

Australia	New Zealand	USA	Sweden	Canada
44.2 pt. 20.9 l.	33.4 pt. 15.8 l.	33.0 pt. 15.6 l.	28.5 pt. 13.5 l.	26.6 pt. 12.6 l.

Each year, the per capita consumption of ice cream in Australia is 44.2 pints (20.9 l). That averages to about 5.28 billion scoops of this frozen favorite for the nation. That means each person would have to eat about 1.7 cups a week during the entire year. Frozen desserts date back to the Roman Empire when people mixed mountain ice with fruit. Ice cream became popular in France, England, and the United States in the eighteenth century. The ice-cream cone was invented in 1904. Today, ice-cream sales total billions of dollars throughout the world.

Country That Consumes the Most Soft Drinks

United States

Americans have an annual per capita soft drink consumption of 51.7 gallons (195.7 l). This means that each person in the country drinks an average of 557 cans of soda each year. Soda accounts for about 25% of all drinks consumed in the United States, and some 17.5 billion gallons (66.2 billion l) are sold annually. Recent studies show that diet sodas, as well as flavored sodas such as cherry, orange, and root beer, are becoming more popular than colas. The country's three top-selling soft drink companies are the Coca-Cola Company, PepsiCo Inc., and Dr Pepper/7 Up.

THE WORLD'S TOP SODA-DRINKING COUNTRIES

Per capita consumption in gallons/liters

USA	Mexico	Norway	Ireland	Canada
51.7 gal. 195.7 l.	33.3 gal. 126.0 l.	32.2 gal. 121.9 l.	32.0 gal. 121.1 l.	30.9 gal. 117.0 l.

Country That Eats the Most Fish

The Maldives

Per capita fish consumption in the Maldives averages 438 pounds (199 kg) each year. This means that all together, the population on this small nation of islands in the north Indian Ocean eats about 148 million pounds (67 million kg) of fish each year. Because the country consists of more than 1,000 coral islands, it makes sense that fishing is one of the top sources of food and income for the people living there. In addition to harvesting fish, Maldivians also eat corn and grains.

THE WORLD'S TOP FISH-EATING COUNTRIES

Per capita consumption in pounds/kilograms

Country	Per capita consumption
Maldives	437.6 lb. / 198.7 kg.
Iceland	198.6 lb. / 90.7 kg.
Portugal	167.8 lb. / 76.2 kg.
Kiribati	166.2 lb. / 75.5 kg.
Japan	140.6 lb. / 63.8 kg.

World's Largest
Meteor Crater

Sudbury Crater

The Sudbury Crater in Ontario, Canada, measures 125 miles (200 km) in diameter. Scientists think it was created when a high-velocity comet the size of Mount Everest crashed into Earth 1.8 billion years ago. The force of this great impact melted a crater in the ground that is about six times the volume of Lake Huron and Lake Ontario combined. Scientists believe that this type of impact happens once every 350 years or so. The Sudbury Crater has suffered some 3.1 miles (5 km) of erosion over the years. The area is frequently used for mining because of the large deposits of copper and nickel found there.

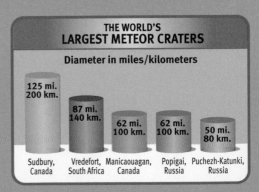

THE WORLD'S LARGEST METEOR CRATERS

Diameter in miles/kilometers

Sudbury, Canada	Vredefort, South Africa	Manicaouagan, Canada	Popigai, Russia	Puchezh-Katunki, Russia
125 mi. 200 km.	87 mi. 140 km.	62 mi. 100 km.	62 mi. 100 km.	50 mi. 80 km.

World's Tallest Mountain

Mount Everest

Towering 29,035 feet (8,850 m) into the air, Mt. Everest's tallest peak is the highest point on Earth. This peak is an unbelievable 5.5 miles (8.8 km) above sea level. Mt. Everest is located in the Himalayas, on the border between Nepal and Tibet. Although it is called Mother Goddess of the Land by Tibetans, the mountain got its official name from surveyor Sir George Everest. In 1953, Sir Edmund Hillary and Tenzing Norgay were the first people to reach the peak.

THE WORLD'S TALLEST MOUNTAINS

Highest point in feet/meters

Mt. Everest, Asia	K2, Asia	Kangchenjunga, Asia	Lhotse, Asia	Makalu Is., Asia
29,035 ft. 8,850 m.	28,250 ft. 8,611 m.	28,208 ft. 8,598 m.	27,923 ft. 8,516 m.	27,824 ft. 8,486 m.

World's Longest
Mountain Chain

The Andes

The Andes extend for about 5,000 miles (8,050 km) through seven countries of South America—Venezuela, Colombia, Ecuador, Peru, Bolivia, Chile, and Argentina. The Andes also have some of the highest peaks in the world, with more than fifty of them measuring above 20,000 feet (6,100 m). Some of the animals found in the Andes include wild horses; vicuñas—members of the camel family; and chinchillas, furry members of the rodent family. The condor—the world's largest bird of prey—also calls these mountains its home.

THE WORLD'S LONGEST MOUNTAIN CHAINS

Length in miles/kilometers

Andes, South America	5,000 mi. 8,050 km.
Trans-Antarctic Mountains, Antarctica	2,200 mi. 3,542 km.
Rocky Mountains, USA	2,000 mi. 3,220 km.
Great Dividing Range, Australia	1,900 mi. 3,059 km.
Himalayas, Asia	1,600 mi. 2,576 km.

World's
Largest Ocean

Pacific

The Pacific Ocean covers almost 64 million square miles (166 million sq km) and reaches 36,200 feet (11,000 m) below sea level at its greatest depth—the Mariana Trench (near the Philippines). In fact, this ocean is so large that it covers about one-third of the planet (more than all of Earth's land put together) and holds more than half of all the seawater on Earth, about 6 sextillion (21 zeros) gallons (23 sextillion l). The United States could fit inside this ocean 18 times! Some of the major bodies of water included in the Pacific are the Bering Sea, the Coral Sea, the Philippine Sea, and the Gulf of Alaska.

THE WORLD'S
LARGEST OCEANS

Maximum area in millions of square miles/square kilometers

Pacific Ocean	Atlantic Ocean	Indian Ocean	Arctic Ocean
64 M sq. mi. 165.7 M sq. km.	31.8 M sq. mi. 82.4 M sq. km.	25.3 M sq. mi. 65.5 M sq. km.	5.4 M sq. mi. 14.0 M sq. km.

181

World's
Largest Desert

The Sahara

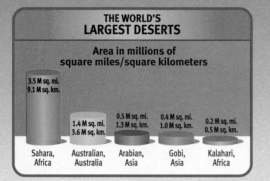

THE WORLD'S LARGEST DESERTS

Area in millions of
square miles/square kilometers

3.5 M sq. mi.
9.1 M sq. km.
Sahara, Africa

1.4 M sq. mi.
3.6 M sq. km.
Australian, Australia

0.5 M sq. mi.
1.3 M sq. km.
Arabian, Asia

0.4 M sq. mi.
1.0 M sq. km.
Gobi, Asia

0.2 M sq. mi.
0.5 M sq. km.
Kalahari, Africa

The Sahara Desert in northern Africa covers approximately 3.5 million square miles (9.1 million sq km). It stretches for 5,200 miles (8,372 km) through the countries of Morocco, Algeria, Tunisia, Libya, Egypt, Mauritania, Mali, Niger, Chad, and Sudan. The Sahara gets very little rainfall—less than 8 inches (20 cm) per year. Date palms and acacias grow near oases. Some of the animals that live in the Sahara include gazelles, antelopes, jackals, foxes, and badgers.

World's
Largest Lake

Caspian Sea

This giant inland body of saltwater stretches for almost 750 miles (1,207 km) from north to south, with an average width of about 200 miles (322 km). All together, it covers an area that's almost the same size as the state of California. The Caspian Sea is located east of the Caucasus Mountains in Central Asia. It is bordered by Iran, Russia, Kazakhstan, Azerbaijan, and Turkmenistan. The Caspian Sea has an average depth of about 550 feet (170 m). It is an important fishing resource, with species including sturgeon, salmon, perch, herring, and carp. Other animals live in the Caspian Sea, including porpoises, seals, and tortoises.

THE WORLD'S LARGEST LAKES

Approximate area in square miles/ square kilometers

Caspian Sea, Asia	Superior, N. America	Victoria, Africa	Huron, N. America	Michigan, N. America
143,205 sq. mi. 370,901 sq. km.	31,820 sq. mi. 82,413 sq. km.	26,570 sq. mi. 68,816 sq. km.	23,010 sq. mi. 59,596 sq. km.	22,400 sq. mi. 58,016 sq. km.

World's
Highest Waterfall

Angel Falls

Angel Falls is the world's highest waterfall at 3,212 feet (979 m). It also holds the record for the longest single drop of any waterfall at 2,648 feet (807 m). Angel Falls is located on the Churun River in the Guiana Highlands of southeastern Venezuela. As the upper river flows over the majestic cliffs, it takes 14 seconds for its water to plunge into the river below. Although rumors of this giant waterfall existed for many years, it was first documented by Ernesto Sanchez La Cruz in 1910. The falls were later named for an American bush pilot, Jimmy Angel, after he spotted them from the air.

THE WORLD'S HIGHEST WATERFALLS

Height in feet/meters

Angel, Venezuela	Tugela, South Africa	Utigard, Norway	Mongefossen, Norway	Yosemite, USA
3,212 ft. 979 m.	3,107 ft. 947 m.	2,625 ft. 800 m.	2,540 ft. 774 m.	2,425 ft. 739 m.

World's Longest River

The Nile

THE WORLD'S LONGEST RIVERS

Total length in miles/kilometers

Nile, Africa	Amazon, S. America	Mississippi-Missouri, N. America	Yangtze, Asia	Yenisei-Angara, Asia
4,145 mi. 6,671 km.	4,000 mi. 6,437 km.	3,740 mi. 6,021 km.	3,720 mi. 5,987 km.	3,650 mi. 5,877 km.

Flowing 4,145 miles (6,671 km), the Nile River in Africa stretches from the tributaries of Lake Victoria in Tanzania and Uganda out to the Mediterranean Sea. Because of varying depths, boats can sail on only about 2,000 miles (3,217 km) of the river. The Nile flows through Rwanda, Uganda, Sudan, and Egypt. The river's water supply is crucial to the existence of these African countries. The Nile's precious water is used to irrigate crops and to generate electricity. The Aswan Dam and the Aswan High Dam—both located in Egypt—are used to store the autumn floodwater for later use.

185

World's
Largest Rock

Ayers Rock

Ayers Rock shoots up 1,100 feet (335 m) above the surrounding desert. The oval-shaped rock is 2.2 miles (3.5 km) long and 1.5 miles (2.4 km) wide. Although it is not the tallest rock, Ayers Rock is the largest by volume. It is located in the southwestern section of the Northern Territory of Australia. Ayers Rock is officially owned by Australia's native people, the Aborigines, who consider the caves at its base to be sacred. The Aborigines lease the giant monolith to the national government so the public may visit it as part of Uluru National Park.

THE WORLD'S LARGEST ROCKS

Height in feet/meters

Ayers Rock, Australia	Dzyarzhynskay, Belarus	Gaizinakalns, Latvia	Seneca Rocks, USA	Coloane Alto, Macau
1,100 ft. 335 m.	1,100 ft. 335 m.	1,024 ft. 312 m.	900 ft. 274 m.	571 ft. 174 m.

World's Largest Island

Greenland

Greenland, located in the North Atlantic Ocean, covers more than 840,000 square miles (2,175,600 sq km). Not including continents, it is the largest island in the world. Its jagged coastline is approximately 24,400 miles (39,267 km) long—about the same distance as Earth's circumference at the equator. Mountain chains are located on Greenland's east and west coasts, and the coastline is indented by fjords, or thin bodies of water bordered by steep cliffs. From north to south, the island stretches for about 1,660 miles (2,670 km). About 700,000 square miles (1,813,000 sq km) of this massive island are covered by a giant ice sheet. Scientists have recently studied these ice sheets to learn more about the history of the world's changing climate.

THE WORLD'S LARGEST ISLANDS

Approximate area in square miles/square kilometers

840,070 sq. mi. 2,175,600 sq. km.	312,190 sq. mi. 808,572 sq. km.	289,961 sq. mi. 751,000 sq. km.	226,674 sq. mi. 587,086 sq. km.	195,926 sq. mi. 507,448 sq. km.
Greenland	New Guinea	Borneo	Madagascar	Baffin Island

World's Highest Island

New Guinea

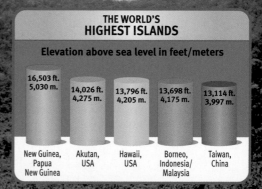

THE WORLD'S HIGHEST ISLANDS

Elevation above sea level in feet/meters

New Guinea, Papua New Guinea	Akutan, USA	Hawaii, USA	Borneo, Indonesia/ Malaysia	Taiwan, China
16,503 ft. 5,030 m.	14,026 ft. 4,275 m.	13,796 ft. 4,205 m.	13,698 ft. 4,175 m.	13,114 ft. 3,997 m.

New Guinea, an island that is part of the nation of Papua New Guinea, sits at an elevation of 16,503 feet (5,030 m) above sea level. It is also the second-largest island in the world. This tropical island has several giant mountain ranges, including the Owen Stanley and the Bismarck Mountains. Jaya Peak, located in Irian Jaya, is the highest point on the island. Some of the creatures that inhabit the island include tree kangaroos, spiny anteaters, and crocodiles. There are also about 650 bird species on the island.

World's Most Harvested Plant

Corn

Each year, the world harvests some 638 million tons (579 M t) of corn. The United States is the world's top corn-growing country, producing about 40% of the total corn crop. It is mostly grown in the country's Midwestern region, known as the Corn Belt. More than half the corn grown in the United States is used for livestock feed, about 25% of the crop is exported, and some 15% is sold as food. Brazil, China, and Mexico also grow a significant amount of corn. In South and Central America, corn is often ground by hand to make tortillas, tamales, and other staple dishes.

THE WORLD'S MOST HARVESTED PLANTS

Millions of tons/metric tons

Corn	Rice	Wheat	Vegetables	Fruits
638.0 M tons 578.8 M t.	589.1 M tons 534.4 M t.	556.4 M tons 504.8 M t.	521.7 M tons 473.3 M t.	472.9 M tons 429.1 M t.

Plants grouped according to the United States Department of Agriculture

World's Largest Seed

Coco de Mer

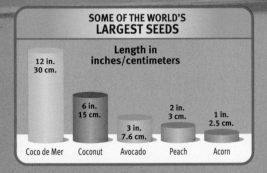

SOME OF THE WORLD'S LARGEST SEEDS

Length in inches/centimeters

12 in.
30 cm.

6 in.
15 cm.

3 in.
7.6 cm.

2 in.
3 cm.

1 in.
2.5 cm.

Coco de Mer   Coconut   Avocado   Peach   Acorn

The giant, dark brown seed of the coco de mer palm tree can reach 12 inches (30 cm) long, measure 3 feet (1 m) in diameter, and weigh up to 40 pounds (18 kg). Only a few thousand seeds are produced each year. Coco de mer trees are found on the island of Praslin in the Seychelles Archipelago of the Indian Ocean. The area where some of the few remaining trees grow has been declared a Natural World Heritage Site in an effort to protect the species from poachers looking for the rare seeds. The tree can grow up to 100 feet (31 m) tall, with leaves measuring 20 feet (6 m) long and 12 feet (3.6 m) wide.

Country That Produces the Most Fruit

China

Each year, China produces more than 74 million tons (67 M t) of fruit—about 14% of the world's total fruit production. The country's fruit crop is worth about $13.2 billion annually. China is the world's top producer of apples and pears, and ranks third in the world for citrus fruit production. The country's orchards total about 21.5 million acres (8.6 M ha)— almost a quarter of the world's orchard land. More than half of China's population works in the agriculture industry.

COUNTRIES THAT PRODUCE THE MOST FRUIT

Millions of tons/metric tons produced annually

China	74.2 M tons / 67.3 M t.
India	47.6 M tons / 43.2 M t.
Brazil	34.3 M tons / 31.1 M t.
USA	30.1 M tons / 27.3 M t.
Mexico	18.6 M tons / 16.9 M t.

World's Largest Flower

Rafflesia

THE WORLD'S LARGEST FLOWERS

Maximum flower size in inches/centimeters

36 in. 91 cm.	19 in. 48 cm.	18 in. 46 cm.	14 in. 36 cm.	10 in. 25 cm.
Rafflesia	Sunflower	Giant Water Lily	Brazilian Dutchman	Magnolia

The giant rafflesia, also known as the "stinking corpse lily," has blossoms that can reach 3 feet (1 m) in diameter and weigh up to 25 pounds (11 kg). Its petals can grow 1.5 feet (0.5 m) long and 1 inch (2.5 cm) thick. There are 16 different species of Rafflesia. This endangered plant is found only in the rain forests of Borneo and Sumatra. It lives inside the bark of host vines and is noticeable only when its flowers break through to blossom. The large, reddish-purple flowers give off a smell similar to rotting meat, which attracts insects to help spread the rafflesia's pollen.

World's Deadliest Plant

Castor Bean Plant

THE WORLD'S DEADLIEST PLANTS

Risk of fatality

Castor Bean	Rosary Bead	Foxglove	Azalea	English Ivy
Extreme	High	High	Medium	Low

The seeds of the castor bean plant contain a protein called ricin. Scientists estimate that ricin is about 6,000 times more poisonous than cyanide and 12,000 times more poisonous than rattlesnake venom. It would take a particle of ricin only about the size of a grain of sand to kill a 160-pound (73-kg) adult. The deadly beans are actually quite pretty and are sometimes used in jewelry. Castor bean plants grow in warmer climates and can reach a height of about 10 feet (3 m). Its leaves can measure up to 2 feet (0.6 m) wide.

World's Tallest Weed

Giant Hogweed

The giant hogweed can grow to a height of 12 feet (3.6 m) and have leaves that measure 3 feet (91 cm) long. That's taller than some trees. The giant hogweed is part of the parsley or carrot family and it has hollow stalks with tiny white flowers. Although it was first brought to America from Asia as an ornamental plant, the hogweed quickly became a pest. Each plant can produce about 50,000 seeds and the weed quickly spreads through its environment.

THE WORLD'S TALLEST WEEDS

Average height in feet/meters

Giant Hogweed	Burdock	Giant Ragweed	Lambsquarters	Bull Thistle
12 ft. 3.6 m.	9 ft. 2.7 m.	8.9 ft. 2.7 m.	7 ft. 2.1 m.	6 ft. 1.8 m.

World's Most
Poisonous Mushroom

Death Cap

THE WORLD'S MOST POISONOUS MUSHROOMS

Ranked 1–5 by likeliness to cause death in humans

Rank	Mushroom
1	Death Cap
2	Destroying Angel
3	Amanita Alba
4	Fly Agaric
5	Deadly Galerina

Among the most dangerous mushrooms are members of the Amanita family, which includes Destroying Angels and the highly dangerous Amanita phalloides, or Death Cap. The Death Cap contains deadly peptide toxins that cause rapid loss of bodily fluids and intense thirst. Within six hours, the poison shuts down the kidneys, liver, and central nervous system, causing coma and—in more than 50% of cases—death. Estimates of the number of poisonous mushroom species range from 80 to 2,000. Most experts agree, however, that at least 100 varieties will cause severe symptoms and even death if eaten.

195

World's Tallest Cactus

Saguaro

Although most saguaro cacti grow to a height of 50 feet (15 m), some have actually reached 75 feet (23 m). That's taller than a seven-story building. Saguaros start out quite small and grow very slowly. A saguaro only reaches about 1 inch (2.5 cm) high during its first 10 years. It will not bloom until it is between 50 and 75 years old. By this time, the cactus has a strong root system that can support about 9 to 10 tons (8 to 9 t) of growth. Its spines can measure up to 2.5 inches (5 cm) long. The giant cactus can be found from southeastern California to southern Arizona.

THE WORLD'S TALLEST CACTI

Height in feet/meters

Saguaro	Organ-Pipe	Opuntia	Cane Cholla	Barrel
50–75 ft. 15–23 m.	40–50 ft. 12–15 m.	33 ft. 10 m.	30 ft. 9 m.	12 ft. 3.7 m.

World's
Largest Leaves

Raffia Palm

Reaching lengths of 65 feet (19.8 m) long, the leaves of these tropical palms measure about the same length as a regulation tennis court. Raffia trees have several stems that can reach heights of 6 to 30 feet (2 to 9 m). When they reach about 50 years of age, raffia palms flower and produce egg-size fruits covered in hard scales. Several products come from these palms, including raffia and floor and shoe polish. Raffia leaves are also used to weave baskets, mats, and hats. These enormous plants are native to Madagascar, but can also be found along Africa's eastern coast.

THE WORLD'S LARGEST LEAVES

Length in feet/meters

Raffia Palm	Fan Palm	Date Palm	Coconut Palm	Oil Palm
65 ft. 19.8 m.	20 ft. 6 m.	18 ft. 5.5 m.	16 ft. 5 m.	13 ft. 4 m.

World's Tallest Tree

California Redwood

California redwoods, which grow in both California and southern Oregon, can reach 385 feet (117.4 m) in height. Their trunks can grow up to 25 feet (7.6 m) in diameter. The tallest recorded redwood stands 385 feet (117.4 m) tall—more than 60 feet (18.3 m) taller than the Statue of Liberty. Some redwoods are believed to be more than 2,000 years old. The trees' thick bark and foliage protect them from natural hazards such as insects and fires.

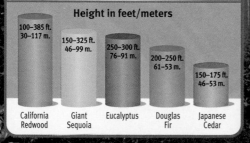

THE WORLD'S
TALLEST TREE SPECIES

Height in feet/meters

- 100–385 ft.
  30–117 m.
  California Redwood
- 150–325 ft.
  46–99 m.
  Giant Sequoia
- 250–300 ft.
  76–91 m.
  Eucalyptus
- 200–250 ft.
  61–53 m.
  Douglas Fir
- 150–175 ft.
  46–53 m.
  Japanese Cedar

Place with the World's Fastest Winds

Mount Washington

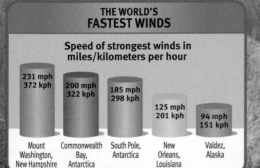

THE WORLD'S FASTEST WINDS

Speed of strongest winds in miles/kilometers per hour

231 mph 372 kph — Mount Washington, New Hampshire
200 mph 322 kph — Commonwealth Bay, Antarctica
185 mph 298 kph — South Pole, Antarctica
125 mph 201 kph — New Orleans, Louisiana
94 mph 151 kph — Valdez, Alaska

In 1934, winds at the top of Mount Washington reached a world record of 231 miles (372 km) per hour—and these gusts were not part of a storm. Normally, the average wind speed at the summit of this mountain is approximately 36 miles (58 km) per hour. Located in the White Mountains of New Hampshire, Mount Washington is the highest peak in New England at 6,288 feet (1,917 m). The treeless summit, which is known for its harsh weather, has an average annual temperature of only 26.5° Fahrenheit (-3.1° C).

World's Driest
Inhabited Place

Aswan

Aswan, Egypt, receives an average rainfall of only .02 inches (.5 mm) per year. In the country's sunniest and southernmost city, summer temperatures can reach a blistering 114° Fahrenheit (46° C). Aswan is located on the west bank of the Nile River. The Aswan High Dam, at 12,565 feet (3,830 m) long, is the city's most famous landmark. It produces the majority of Egypt's power in the form of hydroelectricity. Aswan also has many Pharaonic, Greco-Roman, and Muslim ruins.

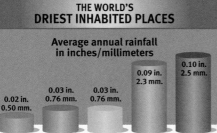

THE WORLD'S DRIEST INHABITED PLACES

Average annual rainfall in inches/millimeters

0.02 in. 0.50 mm.	0.03 in. 0.76 mm.	0.03 in. 0.76 mm.	0.09 in. 2.3 mm.	0.10 in. 2.5 mm.
Aswan, Egypt	Arica, Chile	Luxar, Egypt	Ica, Peru	Wadis Halfa, Sudan

World's Wettest
Inhabited Place

Cherrapunji

The rainfall in Cherrapunji, India, averages 498 inches (1,265 cm) per year. That's enough rain to cover a four-story building! Most of the region's rain falls within a six-month period, during the monsoon season. It's not uncommon for constant rain to pelt the area for two months straight with not even a 10-minute break. During the other six months, the winds change and carry the rain away from Cherrapunji, leaving the ground dry and dusty. Ironically, this causes a drought throughout most of the area.

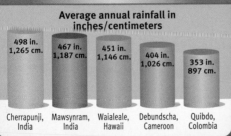

**THE WORLD'S
WETTEST INHABITED PLACES**

Average annual rainfall in
inches/centimeters

498 in. 1,265 cm.	467 in. 1,187 cm.	451 in. 1,146 cm.	404 in. 1,026 cm.	353 in. 897 cm.
Cherrapunji, India	Mawsynram, India	Waialeale, Hawaii	Debundscha, Cameroon	Quibdo, Colombia

World's Hottest
Inhabited Place

Dallol

**THE WORLD'S
HOTTEST INHABITED PLACES**

Average temperature in degrees
Fahrenheit/Celsius

Dallol, Ethiopia	Bangkok, Thailand	Manila, Philippines	Singapore	Assab, Eritrea
94.3° F 34.6° C	90.9° F 32.7° C	89.1° F 31.7° C	87.4° F 30.7° C	86.8° F 30.4° C

Temperatures in Dallol, Ethiopia, in Africa average 94.3° Fahrenheit (34.6° C) throughout the year. On some days it can reach 145° Fahrenheit (62.8° C) in the sun. Dallol is at the northernmost tip of the Great Rift Valley. The Dallol Depression reaches 328 feet (100 m) below sea level, making it the lowest point below sea level that is not covered by water. The area also has several active volcanoes. The only people to inhabit the region are the Afar, who have adapted to the harsh conditions there. For instance, to collect water the women build covered stone piles and wait for condensation to form on the rocks.

World's Coldest
Inhabited Place

Resolute

THE WORLD'S COLDEST INHABITED PLACES

Average temperature in degrees Fahrenheit/Celsius

Resolute, Canada	Eureka, Canada	Ostrov Bol'shoy, Russia	Barrow Point, Alaska	Barter Point, Alaska
-11.6° F -22.8° C	-3.5° F -18.5° C	5.5° F -12.3° C	9.8° F -10.1° C	10.2° F -9.9° C

Canada's hamlet of Resolute averages a chilly annual temperature of -11.6° Fahrenheit (-22.8° C). Located on the northeast shore of Resolute Bay on the south coast of Cornwallis Island, the community is commonly the starting point for expeditions to the North Pole. In the winter it can stay dark for 24 hours, and in the summer it can stay light during the entire night. Only about 200 people brave the climate year-round, but the area is becoming quite popular with tourists.

World's
Greatest Snowfall

Mount Rainier

Between 1971 and 1972, Mount Rainier had a record snowfall of 1,224 inches (3,109 cm). That's enough snow to cover a 10-story building! Located in the Cascade Mountains of Washington state, Mount Rainier is actually a volcano buried under 35 square miles (90.7 sq km) of snow and ice. The mountain, which covers about 100 square miles (259 sq km), reaches a height of 14,410 feet (4,392 m). Its three peaks include Liberty Cap, Point Success, and Columbia Crest. Mt. Rainier National Park was established in 1899.

THE WORLD'S
GREATEST ANNUAL SNOWFALLS

Highest annual snowfall
in inches/centimeters

1,224 in. 3,109 cm.	1,140 in. 2,895 cm.	1,122 in. 2,849 cm.	974 in. 2,474 cm.	964 in. 2,449 cm.
Mount Rainier, Washington, 1971–1972	Mount Baker, Washington, 1998–1999	Paradise Station, Washington, 1971–1972	Thompson Pass, Alaska, 1952–1953	Mount Copeland, British Columbia, 1971–1972

U.S. Records

Alabama to Wyoming

State with the World's Largest
Motorcycle Museum

Alabama

The Barber Vintage Motorsports Museum in Birmingham, Alabama, has a collection of more than 900 motorcycles. Of that 900, the museum only displays about 500 at one time. Some of the bikes that are not on display may be on loan to other museums or exhibits. The other bikes are stored at the museum or they may be continuously rotated into new displays. The Barber has motorcycles from all over the world and from every decade of the twentieth century. The museum opened to the public in 1995 in an effort to preserve the history of motorcycles.

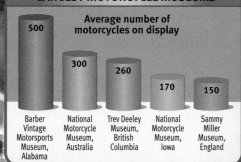

THE WORLD'S LARGEST MOTORCYCLE MUSEUMS

Average number of motorcycles on display

Barber Vintage Motorsports Museum, Alabama	500
National Motorcycle Museum, Australia	300
Trev Deeley Museum, British Columbia	260
National Motorcycle Museum, Iowa	170
Sammy Miller Museum, England	150

State with the Largest
National Park

Alaska

Wrangell-St. Elias National Park in Alaska measures almost 13.2 million acres (5.3 million ha), making it the largest national park in the United States. The Chugach, Wrangell, and St. Elias mountain ranges are all located here, and the area is nicknamed the "mountain kingdom of North America." Many mountain peaks are above 16,000 feet (4,880 m), including Mt. Elias—the United States' second-largest peak—at 18,008 feet (5,492 m). The surrounding area consists of rivers, valleys, and glaciers. There is also a wide variety of wildlife in the region. The area was designated a World Heritage Site in 1980 and was declared a national park later that same year.

THE UNITED STATES' LARGEST NATIONAL PARKS

Millions of acres/hectares

Wrangell-St. Elias, Alaska	13.18 M ac. / 5.26 M ha.
Gates of the Arctic, Alaska	8.47 M ac. / 3.43 M ha.
Denali, Alaska	6.07 M ac. / 2.46 M ha.
Katmai, Alaska	4.73 M ac. / 1.92 M ha.
Death Valley, California	3.37 M ac. / 1.36 M ha.

State with the Country's Sunniest Place

Arizona

The little town of Yuma, Arizona, enjoys bright, sunny days approximately 90% of the year. That means that the sun is shining about 328 days out of each year! Yuma is located in southwestern Arizona near the borders of California and Mexico. Although the temperatures are normally in the 70s year-round, the dry desert air keeps the humidity low. This climate, combined with the waters of the Colorado River, provide Yuma with an excellent environment for its thriving, $633 million-per-year agricultural business.

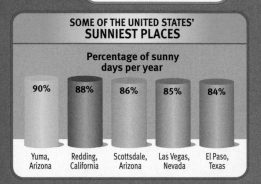

SOME OF THE UNITED STATES' SUNNIEST PLACES

Percentage of sunny days per year

Yuma, Arizona	Redding, California	Scottsdale, Arizona	Las Vegas, Nevada	El Paso, Texas
90%	88%	86%	85%	84%

State with the World's Largest Movie Studio

California

In Los Angeles, California, Universal City's Back Lot measures 415 acres (168 ha), making it the largest movie studio in the world. That's enough land to fit about 20 professional-size football stadiums! The site has 34 soundstages and 561 buildings. The Back Lot has a wide variety of theaters and sets, ranging from street scenes of Paris, London, New York, and the Old West to tropical lagoons. Universal Studios Theme Park is also located here and lets visitors tour soundstages that were used to film hit movies such as *The Scorpion King*, *Shrek*, *Jurassic Park*, and *The Mummy*.

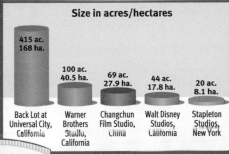

THE WORLD'S LARGEST MOVIE STUDIOS

Size in acres/hectares

- 415 ac. 168 ha. — Back Lot at Universal City, California
- 100 ac. 40.5 ha. — Warner Brothers Studio, California
- 69 ac. 27.9 ha. — Changchun Film Studio, China
- 44 ac. 17.8 ha. — Walt Disney Studios, California
- 20 ac. 8.1 ha. — Stapleton Studios, New York

State with the Largest
Retail Headquarters

Arkansas

Wal-Mart—headquartered in Bentonville, Arkansas—logged $285.2 billion in sales in 2004. The company was founded in 1962 by Arkansas native Sam Walton, who saw his small variety stores grow into giant grocery stores, membership warehouse clubs, and deep-discount warehouse outlets. Wal-Mart currently employs 962,000 workers in the United States and 282,000 workers internationally. Walton's original store in Bentonville now serves as the company's visitor center.

THE UNITED STATES' LARGEST RETAIL HEADQUARTERS

2004 sales, in billions of US dollars

$285.2 B	$73.1 B	$53.8 B	$48.7 B	$36.1 B
Wal-Mart, Arkansas	The Home Depot, Georgia	Kroger, Ohio	Target, Minnesota	Sears Roebuck, Illinois

State's Baseball Team with the Highest Seasonal Attendance

Colorado

In 1993, the seasonal attendance for the Colorado Rockies was an impressive 4.48 million fans. The Rockies finished up their inaugural season in October of the same year with the most wins by a National League expansion team. The Rockies played at Mile High Stadium for their first two years, and during their 135 games there, averaged a crowd of about 57,051 per game. The team moved to Denver's Coors Field in 1995 and proceeded to sell out 203 consecutive games. Since then, the new 76-acre (30.7-ha) ballpark has been a league leader in attendance.

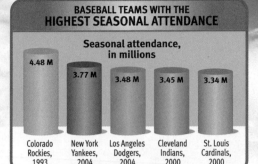

BASEBALL TEAMS WITH THE HIGHEST SEASONAL ATTENDANCE

Seasonal attendance, in millions

Colorado Rockies, 1993	New York Yankees, 2004	Los Angeles Dodgers, 2004	Cleveland Indians, 2000	St. Louis Cardinals, 2000
4.48 M	3.77 M	3.48 M	3.45 M	3.34 M

State with the Oldest Theme Park

Connecticut

Lake Compounce in Bristol, Connecticut, first opened as a picnic park in 1846. The park's first electric roller coaster, the Green Dragon, was introduced in 1914 and cost 10 cents per ride. It was replaced by the WildCat in 1927, and the wooden coaster still operates today. In 1996 the park got a $50 million upgrade, which included the thrilling new roller coaster Boulder Dash. It is the only coaster to be built into a mountainside.

THE UNITED STATES' OLDEST THEME PARKS

Years of establishment

Lake Compounce, Connecticut	Cedar Point, Ohio	Idlewood Park, Pennsylvania	Seabreeze Park, New Jersey	Lakemont Park, Pennsylvania
1846	1870	1878	1879	1894

State with the Largest Pumpkin-Throwing Contest

Delaware

Each year approximately 30,000 people gather in Sussex County, Delaware, for the annual World Championship Punkin Chunkin. More than 70 teams compete during the three-day festival to see who can chuck their pumpkin the farthest. Each team constructs a machine that has a mechanical or compressed-air firing device—no explosives are allowed. The farthest a pumpkin has traveled during the championship is 4,434 feet (1,352 m), or the length of twelve football fields. Each year the festival raises about $100,000 and benefits St. Jude Children's Hospital.

THE UNITED STATES' LARGEST PUMPKIN-THROWING CONTESTS

Spectators

Millsboro, Delaware	Busit, New York	Morton, Illinois	York, Pennsylvania	Salina, Kansas
30,000	5,000	3,500	2,900	1,200

213

State with the
Tallest Hotel

Florida

The Four Seasons Hotel in Miami, Florida, towers a grand 788 feet (241 m) above the surrounding city landscape. This premium hotel has 182 guest rooms and 39 suites. Guests can enjoy a giant spa and health club, a beauty salon, and three swimming pools. The hotel also caters to younger visitors with bedtime milk and cookies, video games, and child-size robes. There is also a Kids for All Seasons program with arts and crafts, movies, and board games.

THE UNITED STATES'
TALLEST HOTELS

Height in feet/meters

Four Seasons, Florida	Westin Peachtree, Georgia	Marriott Renaissance, Michigan	Four Seasons, New York	New York New York, Nevada
788 ft. 241 m.	723 ft. 220 m.	720 ft. 219 m.	682 ft. 208 m.	529 ft. 161 m.

State with the Largest State Sports Hall of Fame

Georgia

THE UNITED STATES' LARGEST STATE SPORTS HALLS OF FAME

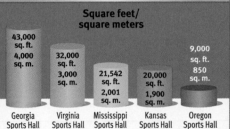

Square feet/ square meters

Georgia Sports Hall of Fame	Virginia Sports Hall of Fame	Mississippi Sports Hall of Fame	Kansas Sports Hall of Fame	Oregon Sports Hall of Fame
43,000 sq. ft. 4,000 sq. m.	32,000 sq. ft. 3,000 sq. m.	21,542 sq. ft. 2,001 sq. m.	20,000 sq. ft. 1,900 sq. m.	9,000 sq. ft. 850 sq. m.

The Georgia Sports Hall of Fame fills 43,000 square feet (3,995 sq m) with memorabilia from Georgia's most accomplished prep, college, amateur, and professional athletes. The hall owns more than 3,000 artifacts and displays about 1,000 of them at a time. Visitors can view films in the theater, learn about the 300 inducted members in the Hall of Fame Corridor, or find out more about an athlete in the extensive research library. Some Hall of Famers include baseball legend Hank Aaron, Olympic basketball great Theresa Edwards, and Super Bowl I champion Bill Curry.

SPORTS HALL OF FAME

State with the Wettest Place

Hawaii

Mount Waialeale, located on the island of Kauai in Hawaii, receives about 460 inches (1,168 cm) of rain each year! Waialeale is located on Alakai Swamp—a plateau on the side of an extinct volcanic depression. It is 5,148 feet (1,569 m) high and is often surrounded by rain clouds. In 1982, Waialeale received 666 inches (1,692 cm) of rain and set an all-time world record. Over time, the constant rain has eroded gorges into the landscape, such as Waimea Canyon, which is 3,000 feet (915 m) deep.

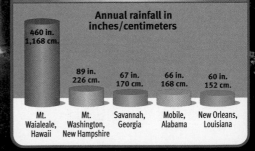

THE UNITED STATES' WETTEST PLACES

Annual rainfall in inches/centimeters

460 in. 1,168 cm.	89 in. 226 cm.	67 in. 170 cm.	66 in. 168 cm.	60 in. 152 cm.
Mt. Waialeale, Hawaii	Mt. Washington, New Hampshire	Savannah, Georgia	Mobile, Alabama	New Orleans, Louisiana

State with the Largest
Raptor Habitat

Idaho

The Snake River Birds of Prey National Conservation Area is located along 81 miles (130 km) of the Snake River in Idaho. This rugged land is home to approximately 2,500 nesting raptors, or birds of prey. The birds stay there from mid-March until late June. Nesting raptor species found here include golden eagles, red-tailed hawks, barn owls, and turkey vultures. In addition to its many bird residents, the area also has one of the largest populations of badgers in the world. Congress designated the 601,053-acre (243,426 ha) habitat a National Conservation Area in August 1993.

THE UNITED STATES' LARGEST RAPTOR HABITATS

Average number of birds during peak times

Snake River, Idaho	Chilkat River, Alaska	Bear Valley, Oregon	Lake Taneycomo, Missouri	Skagit River, Washington
2,500	2,400	1,000	700	350

State with the
Largest Corn Maze

In 2004, the Richardson family of Spring Grove, Illinois, built a corn maze in their crop that covered about 24 acres (9.7 ha). Their maze was a tribute to the Lewis and Clark Expedition, and actually featured three interconnecting mazes. The prairie dog maze and the bison maze each had about 2 miles (3.2 km) of trails, but the Fort Mandan maze stretched on for 6 miles (9.7 km). Even with more than 10 miles (16.1 km) of trails, it only takes about one-third of a mile to solve each maze. There are lots of entrances and exits, so explorers can stop at any point to grab some food or take a rest. And if anyone does feel a bit turned around in all that corn, several employees with walkie-talkies will be happy to go in and locate them.

THE UNITED STATES'
LARGEST CORN MAZES

Area in acres/hectares

24.0 ac. 9.7 ha.	22.0 ac. 8.9 ha.	14.0 ac. 5.7 ha.	12.6 ac. 5.1 ha.	10.0 ac. 4.0 ha.
Spring Grove, Illinois, 2004	Spring Grove, Illinois, 2003	Shakopee, Minnesota, 2003	Lindon, Utah, 1999	Accident, Maryland, 2004

State with the Largest Half Marathon

Indiana

Cars aren't the only things racing in Indianapolis. Each May some 30,000 runners take part in the Indianapolis Life 500 Festival Mini-Marathon. The 13.1-mile (21.1-km) race winds through downtown and includes a lap along the Indianapolis Motor Speedway oval. About 100 musical groups entertain the runners as they complete the course. A giant pasta dinner and after-race party await the runners at the end of the day. The mini-marathon is part of a weekend celebration that centers around the Indianapolis 500 auto race.

THE UNITED STATES'
LARGEST HALF MARATHONS

Number of runners

30,000	Indianapolis Life 500 Festival Mini-Marathon, Indiana
25,000	County Race for the Cure, Michigan
20,000	Boston Athletic Association Half Marathon, Massachusetts
20,000	Rock 'n' Roll Half Marathon, Arizona
18,000	Chicago Half Marathon, Illinois

219

State with the Largest Ice Cream Plant

Iowa

Well's Dairy in LeMars, Iowa, is the largest ice cream plant in the United States, with a factory measuring 500,000 square feet (46,450 sq m). That's about the same size as 106 NBA basketball courts! The family-owned business began in 1913 and delivered milk with a horse-drawn carriage. Today the plant produces its own Blue Bunny ice cream, as well as some Häagen-Dazs products. Well's sold more than $800 million of ice cream and frozen yogurt in 2003. Visitors can tour the Ice Cream Capital of the World Visitor Center in LeMars to see how Blue Bunny frozen treats are made.

THE UNITED STATES' LARGEST ICE CREAM PLANTS

Area in square feet/ square meters

Well's Dairy, Iowa	Marigold Food, Minnesota	Nestlé, Maryland	Dreyer's, California	Ben & Jerry's, Vermont
500,000 sq. ft. 46,450 sq. m.	181,000 sq. ft. 17,000 sq. m.	94,000 sq. ft. 8,700 sq. m.	60,000 sq. ft. 5,600 sq. m.	48,000 sq. ft. 4,500 sq. m.

State with the Largest Ball of Twine

Kansas

In Cawker City, Kansas, there is a giant ball of twine that has a 40-foot (12-m) circumference and weighs more than 17,000 pounds (7,711 kg). The ball is 11 feet (3.4 m) tall and is made up of 1,140 miles (1,835 km) of twine. Frank Stoeber created the ball on his farm in 1953 from twine that he used to wrap hay bales. Cawker City assumed ownership of the twine ball in 1961 and holds a twine-a-thon each year in conjunction with the annual picnic. Thousands of feet of twine are added annually by the town's 800 residents and curious tourists.

THE UNITED STATES' LARGEST BALLS OF TWINE

Approximate weight in pounds/kilograms

17,400 lb. 7,893 kg. — Cawker City, Kansas	17,200 lb. 7,802 kg. — Darwin, Minnesota
12,000 lb. 5,443 kg. — Branson, Missouri	5,300 lb. 2,404 kg. — Jackson, Wyoming

State with the World's
Longest Cave System

Kentucky

With a complex system of tunnels that extends for more than 350 miles (563 km), Kentucky's Mammoth Cave is truly gigantic. Some scientists believe there are still sections of the cave yet to be discovered. This giant underground world has fascinated visitors since prehistoric times. In fact, many ancient artifacts and tools have been located there. Today, about 500,000 people visit the cave each year. They marvel at the stalagmite formations, bottomless pits, and underground rooms. Animals are also drawn to Mammoth Cave. About 130 different species can be found there, including bats, salamanders, and many types of insects.

THE WORLD'S LONGEST CAVE SYSTEMS

Length in miles/kilometers

Mammoth Cave, Kentucky	Optimisti-ceskaja, Ukraine	Jewel Cave, South Dakota	Holloch, Switzerland	Lechuguilla Cave, New Mexico
352 mi. 567 km.	125 mi. 201 km.	108 mi. 174 km.	103 mi. 166 km.	100 mi. 161 km.

State with the Largest
Alligator Population

Louisiana

GATOR XING
NEXT 1/2 MILE

There are approximately 2 million alligators living in Louisiana. That's equal to the number of people living in Houston, Texas—the nation's fourth-largest city! In 1986, Louisiana began an alligator ranching business, which encouraged farmers to raise thousands of the reptiles each year. The farmers must return some alligators to the wild, but they are allowed to sell the rest for profit. Because the alligator business earns about $20 million for Louisiana each year, wetland conservation and alligator protection are strictly enforced. Although alligators can be found in the state's bayous, swamps, and ponds, most live in Louisiana's 3 million acres (1.2 million ha) of coastal marshland.

THE UNITED STATES' LARGEST ALLIGATOR POPULATIONS

Total number of alligators in millions/thousands

Louisiana	Florida	Texas	South Carolina	Georgia
2.0 M	1.6 M	220,000	100,000	80,000

State with the Oldest State Fair

Maine

The first Skowhegan State Fair took place in 1819—a year before Maine officially became a state! Originally sponsored by the Somerset Central Agricultural Society, the fair name became official in 1842. State fairs were very important in the early 1900s. With no agricultural colleges in existence, fairs became the best way for farmers to learn about new agricultural methods and equipment. Today the Skowhegan State Fair features more than 7,000 exhibitors and performers, and people come from all over the country to enjoy concerts, livestock exhibits, and arts and crafts.

THE UNITED STATES' OLDEST STATE FAIRS

Year fair first held

Fair	Year
Skowhegan State Fair, Maine	1819
Three County Fair, Maine	1820
Bangor State Fair, Maine	1851
Brooklyn Fair, Connecticut	1851
Woodstock Fair, Vermont	1862

State with the
Oldest Airport

Maryland

Wright brothers exhibit at
museum at College Park Airport

THE UNITED STATES'
OLDEST AIRPORTS

Year opened

1909	1911	1920	1921	1924
College Park Airport, Maryland	Robertson Airport, Connecticut	Hartness State Airport, Vermont	Bell County Airport, Kentucky	Page Field, Florida

The Wright brothers founded College Park Airport in 1909 to teach Army officers how to fly and it has been in operation ever since. The airport is now owned by the Maryland-National Capital Park and Planning Commission and is on the Register of Historic Places. Many aviation "firsts" occurred at this airport, such as the first woman passenger in the United States (1909), the first test of a bomb-dropping device (1911), the first U.S. Air Mail Service (1918),and the first controlled helicopter flight (1924).

225

State with the Oldest Baseball Stadium

Massachusetts

Fenway Park opened its doors to baseball fans on April 20, 1912. The Boston Red Sox—the park's home team—won the World Series that year. Fenway celebrated again in 2004 when the Sox claimed their second Series win. The park is also the home of the Green Monster—a giant 37-foot (11.3-m) wall with an additional 23-foot (7-m) screen that has plagued home-run hitters since the park first opened. A seat out in the right-field bleachers is painted red to mark where the longest measurable home-run hit inside the park landed. It measured 502 feet (153 m) and was hit by Ted Williams in 1946.

THE UNITED STATES' OLDEST BASEBALL STADIUMS

Year built

1912	1914	1923	1962	1964
Fenway Park, Boston	Wrigley Field, Chicago	Yankee Stadium, New York	Dodger Stadium, Los Angeles	Shea Stadium, New York

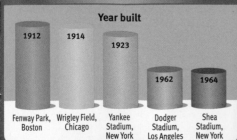

BOSTON RED SOX

State with the World's Largest Indoor Waterfall

Michigan

The 114-foot (34.7-m) waterfall located in the lobby of the International Center in Detroit, Michigan, is the tallest indoor waterfall in the world. The backdrop of this impressive waterfall is a 9,000-square-foot (840-sq-m) slab of marble that was imported from the Greek island of Tinos and installed by eight marble craftsmen. About 6,000 gallons (27,276 l) of water spill down the waterfall each minute. That's the liquid equivalent of 80,000 cans of soda! Visitors can see this $1.5 million creation as they stroll through the International Center, which also houses many retail shops.

THE WORLD'S LARGEST INDOOR WATERFALLS

Height in feet/meters

International Center, Michigan	Trump Tower, New York	Mohegan Sun, Connecticut	Orchid Hotel, India	Casino Windsor, Michigan
114 ft. 34.7 m.	90 ft. 27.4 m.	85 ft. 26.1 m.	70 ft. 21.3 m.	60 ft. 18.3 m.

State with the Largest
Hockey Stick

Minnesota

There is a hockey stick in the town of Eveleth, Minnesota, that measures 110 feet (33.5 m) long and weighs 5 tons (4.5 t). It was crafted in the exact same way a normal-size hockey stick would be, except the job called for about 3,000 times more wood. To transport the giant stick to Minnesota, the delivery truck had a state police escort to block some roads and intersections along the way. The giant hockey stick is positioned next to a 700-pound (318-kg) hockey puck. The stick was dedicated to the hockey players of the past, present, and future, and to the spirit of hockey in Eveleth.

THE UNITED STATES' LARGEST SPORTS EQUIPMENT MONUMENTS

Height in feet/meters

110 ft. 33.5 m.	120 ft. 36.6 m.	24 ft. 7.3 m.	18 ft. 5.5 m.	12 ft. 3.6 m.
Hockey Stick, Minnesota	Baseball Bat, Kentucky	Bowling Pin, New Jersey	Arrows, Colorado	Soccer Ball, Missouri

State with the
Most Catfish

Mississippi

There are 680 million catfish in Mississippi—more than 72% of the world's farm-raised supply. That's almost enough to give every person in the state 235 fish each. The state's residents are quite proud of their successful fish industry. The World Catfish Festival is held every April in the town of Belzoni—also known as the Catfish Capital of the World. There, festival-goers can tour the Catfish Institute, which details the journey of the catfish from the pond to the plate.

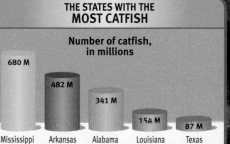

THE STATES WITH THE MOST CATFISH

Number of catfish, in millions

Mississippi	Arkansas	Alabama	Louisiana	Texas
680 M	482 M	341 M	154 M	87 M

State with the Largest
Outdoor Musical Theater

Missouri

THE UNITED STATES' LARGEST OUTDOOR MUSICAL THEATERS

Square feet/square meters

The Muny, Missouri	Alpine Valley Music Theater, Wisconsin	Journal Pavilion, New Mexico	Miller Outdoor Theater, Texas	Starlight Theater, Missouri
80,000 sq. ft. 7,432 sq. m.	55,000 sq. ft. 5,100 sq. m.	45,000 sq. ft. 4,200 sq. m.	37,000 sq. ft. 3,500 sq. m.	12,000 sq. ft. 1,100 sq. m.

The Municipal Theatre in St. Louis—affectionately known as The Muny—is the nation's largest outdoor theater, with 80,000 square feet (7,432 sq m) and 11,500 seats—about the same size as a regulation soccer field. Amazingly, construction on the giant theater was completed in just 42 days. The theater opened in 1917 with a production of Verdi's *Aïda*, and the best seats cost only $1.00. Today, the Muny offers classic Broadway shows each summer, with past productions including *Cats*, *The Music Man*, and *Annie*.

State with the Oldest
National Monument

Montana

The Little Big Horn Battlefield National Monument, located near Crow Agency, Montana, was first designated a national cemetery in 1879. A memorial was built on Last Stand Hill two years later to commemorate the Seventh Cavalry soldiers who died there. The Battle of the Little Big Horn took place on June 25 and 26, 1876. General George Custer and the Seventh Cavalry were defeated by the Lakota, Cheyenne, and Arapaho. Today, the memorial complex has a museum, hiking trails, and a research library.

THE UNITED STATES'
OLDEST NATIONAL MONUMENTS

Date established

Jan. 29, 1881	March 2, 1889	Sept. 24, 1906	Dec. 8, 1906	Dec. 8, 1906
Little Big Horn Battlefield, Montana	Casa Grande Ruins, Arizona	Devil's Tower, Wyoming	El Morro, New Mexico	Montezuma Castle, Arizona

231

State with the Most Sandhill Cranes

Nebraska

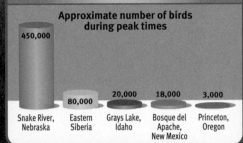

THE WORLD'S LARGEST SANDHILL CRANE POPULATIONS

Approximate number of birds during peak times

Snake River, Nebraska	450,000
Eastern Siberia	80,000
Grays Lake, Idaho	20,000
Bosque del Apache, New Mexico	18,000
Princeton, Oregon	3,000

For approximately five weeks each spring, Nebraska is the resting spot for 400,000 to 500,000 sandhill cranes. That's about 75% of the world's sandhill crane population! As part of their annual migration, these birds arrive from Texas, New Mexico, California, and Arizona to feed and rest along a 150-mile (241-km) stretch of the Platte River between Grand Isle and Sutherland. The Crane Meadows Nature Center is located along the Central Flyway and is a prime location to view and learn more about these cranes. The residents of this area celebrate the cranes' arrival during the annual Spring Wing Ding celebration.

State with the Largest
Glass Sculpture

Nevada

THE WORLD'S LARGEST
GLASS SCULPTURES

Length in feet/meters

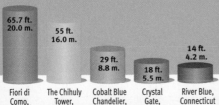

65.7 ft. 20.0 m.	55 ft. 16.0 m.	29 ft. 8.8 m.	18 ft. 5.5 m.	14 ft. 4.2 m.
Fiori di Como, Nevada	The Chihuly Tower, Oklahoma	Cobalt Blue Chandelier, Washington	Crystal Gate, Bahamas	River Blue, Connecticut

Fiori di Como—the breathtaking chandelier at the Bellagio Hotel in Las Vegas, Nevada—measures 65.7 feet by 29.5 feet (20 m by 9 m). Created by Dale Chihuly, the handblown glass chandelier consists of more than 2,000 discs of colored glass. Each disc is about 18 inches (45.7 cm) wide and hangs about 20 feet (6.1 m) overhead. Together, these colorful discs look like a giant field of flowers. The chandelier required about 10,000 pounds of steel (4,540 kg) and 40,000 pounds (18,160 kg) of handblown glass.

233

State with the Oldest
Covered Bridge

New Hampshire

The Haverhill-Bath Covered Bridge in New Hampshire was completed in 1832 and crosses the Ammonoosuc River to connect the towns of Haverhill and Bath. It has a two-lane span of 278 feet (85 m). Until 1999, the bridge had been open to cars and trucks. But because of its narrow width and the high cost of renovating the bridge, it is now only open to pedestrians and bicyclists. Today, New Hampshire has approximately 55 remaining covered bridges, but the number is shrinking due to deterioration from cold, harsh weather, vandalism, and neglect.

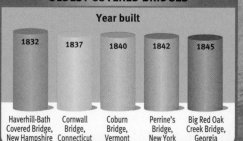

THE UNITED STATES'
OLDEST COVERED BRIDGES

Year built

Haverhill-Bath Covered Bridge, New Hampshire	Cornwall Bridge, Connecticut	Coburn Bridge, Vermont	Perrine's Bridge, New York	Big Red Oak Creek Bridge, Georgia
1832	1837	1840	1842	1845

State with the World's
Longest Boardwalk

New Jersey

**THE WORLD'S
LONGEST BOARDWALKS**

Length in miles/kilometers

- 4.0 mi. 6.4 km. — Atlantic City, New Jersey
- 3.0 mi. 4.8 km. — Coney Island, New York
- 2.5 mi. 4.0 km. — FDR Boardwalk, New York
- 2.0 mi. 3.2 km. — Jarzoo Boardwalk, Sweden
- 1.0 mi 1.6 km. — Wilderness on Wheels, Colorado

The famous boardwalk in Atlantic City, New Jersey, stretches for 4 miles (6.4 km) along the beach. Combined with the adjoining boardwalk in Ventnor, the length increases to just under 6 miles (9.7 km). The 60-foot- (18-m) wide boardwalk opened on June 26, 1870. It was the first boardwalk built in the United States, and was designed to keep sand out of the tourists' shoes. Today the boardwalk is filled with amusement parks, shops, restaurants, and hotels. About 35 million people take a stroll along the walk each year.

State with the World's Largest
Balloon Festival

New Mexico

Each October, approximately 1,000 hot-air and gas-filled balloons take part in the Kodak Albuquerque International Balloon Fiesta in the skies over New Mexico. This event draws balloons from around the world, and is often seen in more than 50 countries. The festival takes place in the 350-acre (142-ha) Balloon Fiesta State Park. The Balloon Fiesta has also hosted some prestigious balloon races, including the Gordon Bennett Cup (1993), World Gas Balloon Championship (1994), and the America's Challenge Gas Balloon Race (1995).

THE WORLD'S LARGEST BALLOON FESTIVALS

Approximate number of balloons

Albuquerque, New Mexico	1,000
Gallup, New Mexico	200
Greenville, South Carolina	150
Gatineau, Canada	150
Scottsdale, Arizona	150

State with the World's Largest Cinema

New York

Radio City Music Hall in New York City is the world's largest cinema with 5,910 seats. Its marquee is a city block long, and the auditorium measures 84 feet (25.6 m) high—about half the height of the Statue of Liberty. The organ in the theater—known as the Mighty Wurlitzer—has pipes that reach up to 32 feet (9.7 m) high and are housed in eleven separate rooms. The theater opened in December 1932 and was originally known as The Showplace of the Nation. Since then, more than 300 million people have come to the Music Hall to see concerts, stage shows, movies, and special events. Radio City Music Hall has hosted more than 700 movie premieres, including *King Kong*, *Breakfast at Tiffany's*, *Mary Poppins*, and *The Lion King*.

THE WORLD'S LARGEST CINEMAS

Seating capacity

Cinema	Seating capacity
Radio City Music Hall, New York	5,910
Kodak Theatre, California	3,500
New York State Theater, New York	2,755
Verizon Wireless Theater, Texas	2,400
Mahaffey Theater, Florida	2,000

State with the Oldest
State University

North Carolina

The University of North Carolina (UNC) was founded in 1789 but did not accept its first student at Chapel Hill until February 1795 because of a lack of funding. By the following month, the university consisted of 2 buildings, 2 professors, and 41 students. This makes UNC the only university in the United States to graduate students in the 18th century. Today, the University of North Carolina has more than 15,000 undergraduates and 2,400 faculty. The university has 16 campuses in the state, including Chapel Hill, Charlotte, Wilmington, and Asheville.

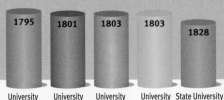

THE UNITED STATES'
OLDEST PUBLIC UNIVERSITIES

Year established

University of North Carolina	University of Vermont	University of Georgia	University of South Carolina	State University of New York, New Paltz
1795	1801	1803	1803	1828

State with the Largest
Hoofed Mammal

North Dakota

THE UNITED STATES'
LARGEST HOOFED MAMMAL STATUES

Approximate size in feet/meters

38 ft. 11.6 m.	30 ft. 9 m.	26 ft. 7.9 m.	22 ft. 6.7 m.
Salem Sue, North Dakota	Bull, Iowa	Buffalo, North Dakota	Dala Horse Minnesota

"Salem Sue" weighs about 12,000 pounds (5,443 kg) and stands 38 feet (11.6 m) above the fields that surround her. Salem Sue measures 50 feet (15m) long and is made out of fiberglass. The world's largest Holstein was built in 1974 and cost approximately $40,000. She was funded by area farmers, businesspeople, and local residents to celebrate New Salem's success in the dairy industry. The New Salem Lions organized the initial project and today continue to keep up Salem Sue's maintenance. Salem Sue also has a regional friend—North Dakota has the world's largest buffalo statue.

State with the World's Largest
Twins Gathering

Ohio

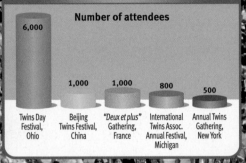

THE WORLD'S LARGEST TWINS GATHERINGS

Number of attendees

6,000	1,000	1,000	800	500
Twins Day Festival, Ohio	Beijing Twins Festival, China	"Deux et plus" Gathering, France	International Twins Assoc. Annual Festival, Michigan	Annual Twins Gathering, New York

Each August, the town of Twinsburg, Ohio, hosts about 6,000 twins at its annual Twins Day Festival. Both identical and fraternal twins from around the world participate, and many dress alike. The twins take part in games, parades, and contests, such as the oldest identical twins and the twins with the widest combined smile. Since twins from ages 90 to just 11 days old have attended, there are special twin programs for all age groups. The event began in 1976 in honor of Aaron and Moses Wilcox, twin brothers who inspired the city to adopt its name in 1817.

State with the Largest Military Museum

Oklahoma

Located in Oklahoma City, Oklahoma, the 45th Infantry Division Museum is spread over 15 acres (6.1 ha). Thousands of exhibits and artifacts related to the military history of Oklahoma are displayed in the museum's seven buildings. Galleries feature artifacts that take visitors through World War II and Desert Storm. The museum also features 200 of Bill Mauldin's original "Willie and Joe" cartoons about two riflemen in World War II, the Reaves Collection of military weapons, and Korean-era artillery. The outdoor Military Park has more than 50 military vehicles, aircraft, and artillery. Thunderbird Monument is also on the grounds and honors veterans of World War II and Korea.

THE UNITED STATES' LARGEST MILITARY MUSEUMS

Approximate size in acres/hectares

- 15 ac. 6.1 ha. — 45th Infantry Museum, Oklahoma
- 10 ac. 4 ha. — Patton Museum of Cavalry, Kentucky
- 6 ac. 2.4 ha. — Army Transportation Museum, Virginia
- 1.6 ac. 0.65 ha. — San Diego Aerospace Museum, California
- 0.1 ac. 0.05 ha. — Wisconsin National Guard Museum

State with the World's
Longest Sea Cave

Oregon

Sea Lion Cave, located on the Pacific coast of Oregon, reaches a length of 360 feet (110 m). That's the same length as a football field. The cave is also 120 feet (37 m) from floor to ceiling. Sea Lion Cave began to form approximately 25 million years ago. One of the most amazing things about this natural wonder is its inhabitants. Two of the most common species of sea lions found in and around the caves include the Steller sea lion and the California sea lion. California gulls, western gulls, and herring gulls also live here. During the summer, gray whales can be seen feeding just offshore.

THE WORLD'S LONGEST SEA CAVES

Length in feet/meters

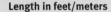

Sea Lion Cave, Oregon	Fingal's Cave, Scotland	Hamnsund-helleren, Norway	Smoo Cave, Scotland	Wookey Hole, England
360 ft. 110 m.	250 ft. 76 m.	230 ft. 70 m.	223 ft. 68 m.	200 ft. 61 m.

State with the Oldest Zoo

Pennsylvania

Although the Philadelphia Zoo was chartered in 1859, it didn't officially open its doors to the public until 1874 because of the Civil War. As the zoo grew, it continued to set records—it had the first adult male elephant ever exhibited in the United States (1888), the first orangutan birth in a U.S. zoo (1928), and the first zoo birth of cheetahs in the world (1956). Today, the Philadelphia Zoo cares for more than 1,600 animals from around the world. Some of its exhibits include the Rare Animal Conservation Center, Peco Primate Reserve, Bird Valley, and Dodge Wild Earth. The large Animal Health Center Is equipped to treat animals ranging from hummingbirds to polar bears.

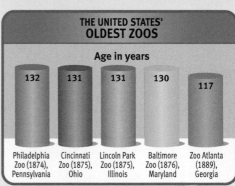

THE UNITED STATES'
OLDEST ZOOS

Age in years

Philadelphia Zoo (1874), Pennsylvania	Cincinnati Zoo (1875), Ohio	Lincoln Park Zoo (1875), Illinois	Baltimore Zoo (1876), Maryland	Zoo Atlanta (1889), Georgia
132	131	131	130	117

State with the Oldest* Carousel

*Continually operating

Rhode Island

THE UNITED STATES' OLDEST CONTINUALLY OPERATING CAROUSELS

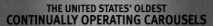

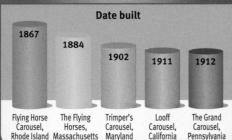

Date built

1867	1884	1902	1911	1912
Flying Horse Carousel, Rhode Island	The Flying Horses, Massachusetts	Trimper's Carousel, Maryland	Looff Carousel, California	The Grand Carousel, Pennsylvania

The Flying Horse Carousel in Watch Hill, Rhode Island, was manufactured by the Charles W. Dare Company of New York in 1867. A traveling carnival was passing through the popular summer vacation spot and could no longer transport the carousel. The Flying Horse Carousel is unique because the horses are attached from chains on the ceiling, not by poles on the floor. Each horse is hand-carved from a single piece of wood. The horses' tails and manes are made of real horsehair, and their saddles are made of leather.

State with the Oldest
Landscaped Gardens

South Carolina

The geometrical garden patterns in Middleton Place Gardens were designed by Henry Middleton in 1741 and were modeled after the gardens at the Palace of Versailles in France. They were first opened to the public in the 1920s. Today, the gardens on this 65-acre (26.3 ha) Charleston plantation are laid out in almost the same fashion as when they were planted more than 250 years ago. Some of the plants that are featured at Middleton Place Gardens include camellias, daffodils, magnolias, jasmine, columbine, and hydrangea.

THE UNITED STATES' OLDEST LANDSCAPED GARDENS

Year established

1741	1853	1891	1907	1932
Middleton Place Gardens, South Carolina	Missouri Botanical Gardens, Missouri	New York Botanical Gardens, New York	Longwood Gardens, Pennsylvania	Hershey Gardens, Pennsylvania

State with the World's Largest Portrait Bust

South Dakota

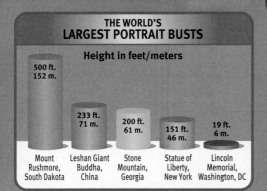

THE WORLD'S LARGEST PORTRAIT BUSTS

Height in feet/meters

500 ft. 152 m.	233 ft. 71 m.	200 ft. 61 m.	151 ft. 46 m.	19 ft. 6 m.
Mount Rushmore, South Dakota	Leshan Giant Buddha, China	Stone Mountain, Georgia	Statue of Liberty, New York	Lincoln Memorial, Washington, DC

Located in the Black Hills of South Dakota, Mount Rushmore National Memorial features a 500-foot-high (152 m) portrait bust of four American presidents. The faces of George Washington, Thomas Jefferson, Abraham Lincoln, and Theodore Roosevelt are each about 60 feet (18.3 m) high. Gutzon Borglum began to carve this monument in 1927, but the work took 14 years to complete. The entire project cost only about $1 million. More than 2 million people visit the memorial each year.

State with the World's Largest Freshwater Aquarium

Tennessee

THE WORLD'S LARGEST FRESHWATER AQUARIUMS

Size in square feet/ square meters

Tennessee Aquarium, Tennessee, USA	The Freshwater Center, Denmark	Great Lakes Aquarium, Minnesota, USA	Aquarium of the Lakes, Britain	Gifu Freshwater Aquarium, Japan
130,000 sq. ft. 12,077 sq. m.	91,494 sq. ft. 8,500 sq. m.	62,382 sq. ft. 5,795 sq. m.	49,514 sq. ft. 4,600 sq. m.	46,284 sq. ft. 4,300 sq. m.

The Tennessee Aquarium in Chattanooga is an impressive 130,000 square feet (12,077 sq m), making it the largest freshwater aquarium in the world. An additional 60,000-square-foot (5,574-sq-m) area will open in spring 2005. Permanent features in the aquarium include an IMAX theater, Discovery Hall, and an Environmental Learning Lab. Some of the aquarium's 9,000 animals include baby alligators, paddlefish, lake sturgeon, seadragons, and pipefish. And to feed all of these creatures, the aquarium goes through 12,000 crickets, 33,300 worms, and 1,200 pounds (545 kg) of seafood each month!

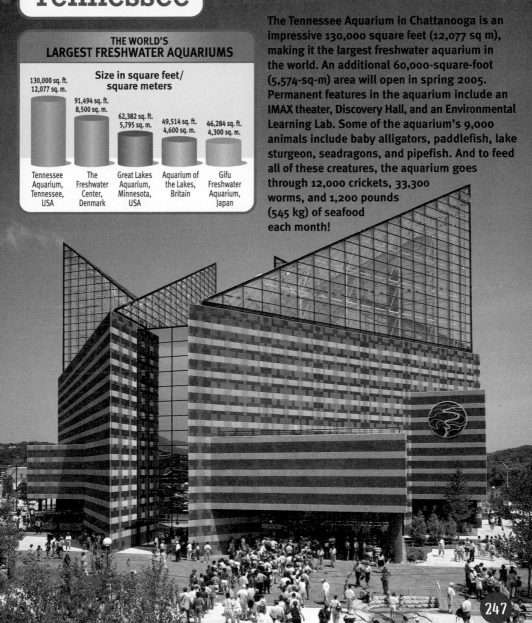

247

State with the Biggest Ferris Wheel

Texas

The State Fair of Texas boasts the nation's largest ferris wheel. Called the Texas Star, this colossal wheel measures 212 feet (64.6 m) high. That's taller than a 20-story building! The Texas Star was built in Italy and shipped to Texas for its debut at the 1986 fair. The Texas Star is just one of the 70 rides featured at the fair. The three-week-long State Fair of Texas is held in the fall, and the giant ferris wheel is not the only grand-scale item there. Big Tex, a 52-foot- (15.9-m) tall cowboy, is the fair's mascot and the biggest cowboy in the United States.

THE UNITED STATES' LARGEST FERRIS WHEELS

Height of wheel in feet/meters

Texas Star, Texas	Colossus, Massachusetts	Giant Wheel, Ohio	Navy Pier Ferris Wheel, Illinois	Six Flags Ferris Wheel, Kentucky
212 ft. 64.6 m.	150 ft. 45.8 m.	150 ft. 45.8 m.	150 ft. 45.8 m.	150 ft. 45.8 m.

State with the World's Largest
Human-Made Hole

Utah

Bingham Canyon—a working mine in the Oquirrh Mountains—is the largest human-made hole in the world. It measures 2.5 miles (4 km) wide and 0.5 miles (0.8 km) deep. It is so large that astronauts can even see it from space. Miners first began digging in the area in 1903. Today approximately 63 million tons (57 million t) of ore and 123 million tons (112 million t) of waste are removed from the canyon each year. Bingham Canyon is one of the largest copper mining operations in the world. In 2003, more than 281,000 tons (254,867 t) of copper were produced. Silver and gold are also mined there.

THE WORLD'S LARGEST HUMAN-MADE HOLES

Width of opening in miles/kilometers

Bingham Canyon, Utah	Hull-Rust Mahoning Mine, Minnesota	Berkley Pit, Minnesota	Big Hole Diamond Mine, South Africa	Rubislaw Quarry, Scotland
2.5 mi. 4.0 km.	2.0 mi. 3.2 km.	1.1 mi. 1.8 km.	0.5 mi. 0.8 km.	0.1 mi. 0.16 km.

State That Produces the
Most Maple Syrup

Vermont

Maple syrup production in Vermont totaled 500,000 gallons (1,892,706 l) in 2004 and accounted for about 33% of the United States' total yield that year. There are about 2,000 maple syrup producers in Vermont, and the annual production generates more than $13.9 million. It takes about 5 tree taps to collect enough maple sap—approximately 40 gallons (150 l)—to produce just 1 gallon (3.79 l) of syrup. Vermont maple syrup is also made into maple sugar, maple cream, and maple candies.

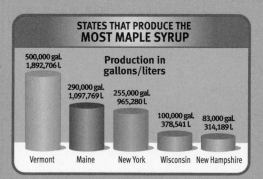

STATES THAT PRODUCE THE MOST MAPLE SYRUP

Production in gallons/liters

500,000 gal.
1,892,706 L

290,000 gal.
1,097,769 L

255,000 gal.
965,280 L

100,000 gal.
378,541 L

83,000 gal.
314,189 L

Vermont   Maine   New York   Wisconsin   New Hampshire

Birthplace of the
Most Presidents

Virginia

The Commonwealth of Virginia has earned the nickname "the Mother of Presidents" because eight of America's chief executives were born there. These presidents are George Washington (1st; 1789–1797), Thomas Jefferson (3rd; 1801–1809), James Madison (4th; 1809–1817), James Monroe (5th; 1817–1825), William Henry Harrison (9th; 1841), John Tyler (10th; 1841–1845), Zachary Taylor (12th; 1849–1850), and Woodrow Wilson (28th; 1913–1921). Since the first colony was founded here in 1607, Virginia has played a big part in the nation's political development. Each year many tourists visit Virginia's historical sites to learn more about the country's past.

**BIRTHPLACES OF THE
MOST PRESIDENTS**

Virginia	Ohio	Massachusetts	New York	Texas
8	7	4	4	3

*Mount Vernon, former home of
President George Washington*

State That Produces the
Most Apples

Washington

The state of Washington produces about 5.4 billion pounds (2.4 billion kg) of apples in just one year. That's enough to give every person in the country 18.5 pounds (8.4 kg) of apples annually. The Columbia Basin is where most of the state's produce is grown. Located in the central part of Washington, its fertile, well-drained soil is ideal for apple trees. In the United States, about one-half of the annual apple crop is sold as fresh fruit. Another one-fifth of the apple crop is used for juice, jelly, apple butter, and vinegar.

THE UNITED STATES'
TOP APPLE-PRODUCING STATES

Apples produced, in billions and millions of pounds/kilograms

Washington	New York	Michigan	California	Pennsylvania
5.4 B lbs. 2.4 B kg.	1.1 B lbs. 0.5 B kg.	690 M lbs. 313 M kg.	440 M lbs. 200 M kg.	416 M lbs. 189 M kg.

State with the Longest
Steel Arch Bridge

West Virginia

THE UNITED STATES' LONGEST
STEEL ARCH BRIDGES

**Length of main span
in feet/meters**

1,700 ft. 518 m.	1,675 ft. 511 m.	1,255 ft. 383 m.	1,080 ft. 329 m.	1,038 ft. 316 m.
New River Gorge Bridge, West Virginia	Bayonne Bridge, New Jersey	Fremont Bridge, Oregon	Roosevelt Lake Bridge, Arizona	Hell Gate Bridge, New York

With a main span of 1,700 feet (518 m) and a weight of about 88 million pounds (40 million kg), the New River Gorge Bridge in Fayetteville, West Virginia, is the longest and largest steel arch bridge in the United States. It is approximately 875 feet (267 m) above the New River and is the second-highest bridge in the United States. After three years of construction, the bridge was completed in 1977. This $37-million structure is the focus of Bridge Day—a statewide annual festival that commemorates its building. This is the only day that the New River Gorge Bridge is open to pedestrians.

State with the Country's
Largest Water Park

Wisconsin

Noah's Ark in Wisconsin Dells sprawls for 70 acres (28.4 ha) and includes 36 waterslides. One of the most popular—Dark Voyage—takes visitors on a twisting rapids ride in the dark. The ride can pump 8,000 gallons (30,283 l) of water a minute. Visitors can also enjoy two wave pools, two mile-long "endless" rivers, and four children's play areas. It takes 5 million gallons (19 million l) of water—the equivalent of more than 14 Olympic swimming pools—to fill all the pools and operate the 3 miles (4.8 km) of waterslides. Also spread throughout the giant water complex are 4,000 lounge chairs, 5,000 inner tubes, and 600 picnic tables.

254

THE UNITED STATES'
LARGEST WATER PARKS

Size in acres/hectares

70 ac. 28.4 ha.	66 ac. 26.7 ha.	65 ac. 26.3 ha.	60 ac. 24.3 ha.	60 ac. 24.3 ha.
Noah's Ark, Wisconsin	Blizzard Beach, Florida	Schlitterbahn Beach Waterpark, Texas	Oceans of Fun, Missouri	Six Flags Splash Town, Texas

State with the Oldest National Park

Wyoming

The U.S. Congress designated the Yellowstone region of eastern Wyoming as the world's first national park in March 1872. Many geological features found at Yellowstone are unusual. In fact, the park has more than 10,000 hot springs and 200 geysers—the greatest concentration of geothermal features in the world. Yellowstone is also known for its wildlife. Bison, bighorn sheep, moose, black bears, wolves, and many species of birds and fish can be found in the park. This giant preserve covers almost 2.2 million acres (0.9 M ha) of mostly undeveloped land.

THE UNITED STATES' OLDEST NATIONAL PARKS

Year founded

1872	1890	1890	1890	1899
Yellowstone, Wyoming, Montana, Idaho	Sequoia, California	Kings Canyon, California	Yosemite, California	Mt. Rainier, Washington

255

Human-Made Records

Constructions • Travel • Transportation

World's Highest
Suspension Bridge

Royal Gorge

THE WORLD'S HIGHEST SUSPENSION BRIDGES

Height in feet/meters

- 1,053 ft. 321 m. — Royal Gorge, USA
- 507 ft. 155 m. — Tacoma Narrows, USA
- 318 ft. 97 m. — Akashi-Kaikyo, Japan
- 228 ft. 69 m. — Verrazano-Narrows, USA
- 220 ft. 67 m. — Golden Gate, USA

The Royal Gorge Bridge—in Canon City, Colorado—spans the Arkansas River 1,053 feet (321 m) above the water. The bridge is 1,260 feet (384 m) long and 18 feet (5 m) wide. About 1,000 tons (907 t) of steel make up the bridge's floor, which can hold in excess of 2 million pounds (907,200 kg). The cables weigh about 300 tons (272 t) each. The bridge took just five months to complete in 1929, at a cost of $350,000.

World's Longest Suspension Bridge

Akashi-Kaikyo

This giant suspension bridge connects Maiko, Tarumi Ward, in Kobe City to Matsuho, Awaji Town, in Japan. All together, the bridge spans the Akashi Strait for 2 miles (3 km) in Tsuna County on the Japanese island of Awajishima. Built in 1998, the structure's main span is a record-breaking 6,529 feet (1,990 m) long with cables supporting the 100,000-ton (90,700-t) bridge below. Each cable is made up of 290 strands of wire. More than 186,000 miles (30,000 km) of wire was used for the project—enough to circle Earth 7.5 times! The main tower soars approximately 984 feet (300 m) into the air.

THE WORLD'S LONGEST SUSPENSION BRIDGES

Length of main span in feet/meters

Akashi-Kaikyo, Japan	Izmit Bay, Turkey	Storebaelt, Denmark	Humber Estuary, UK	Jiangyin, China
6,529 ft. 1,990 m.	5,472 ft. 1,668 m.	5,328 ft. 1,624 m.	4,626 ft. 1,410 m.	4,544 ft. 1,385 m.

World's
Tallest Hotel

Burj Al Arab

THE WORLD'S TALLEST HOTELS

Height in feet/meters

1,053 ft. 321 m.	1,046 ft. 319 m.	1,014 ft. 309 m.	985 ft. 300 m.	858 ft. 262 m.
Burj Al Arab, UAE	Baiyoke II Tower, Thailand	Emirates Hotel Tower, UAE	Yukong, North Korea	Emirates Tower II, UAE

The Burj Al Arab—or Tower of the Arabs—in Dubai, United Arab Emirates (UAE) stands an incredible 1,053 feet (321 m) above the ground. This makes it the world's tallest hotel, as well as the sixteenth-tallest building in the world. The hotel is shaped like a ship's billowing sail and is a part of the Jumeirah Beach resort. It was built in 1999 on a human-made island in the Arabian Gulf. Guests at the Burj Al Arab can choose from 202 luxury suites. Kids staying at the hotel will enjoy the family pool with an artificial beach and waterslide. Suites in this amazing hotel start at around $1,000 per night.

World's Tallest Habitable Building

Taipei 101

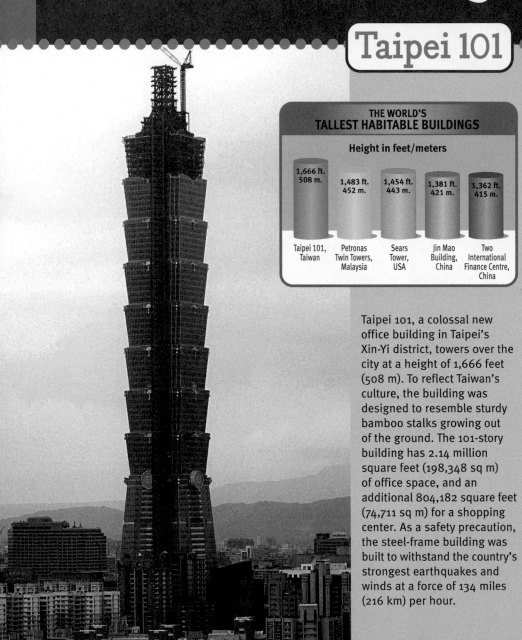

THE WORLD'S TALLEST HABITABLE BUILDINGS

Height in feet/meters

1,666 ft. 508 m.	1,483 ft. 452 m.	1,454 ft. 443 m.	1,381 ft. 421 m.	1,362 ft. 415 m.
Taipei 101, Taiwan	Petronas Twin Towers, Malaysia	Sears Tower, USA	Jin Mao Building, China	Two International Finance Centre, China

Taipei 101, a colossal new office building in Taipei's Xin-Yi district, towers over the city at a height of 1,666 feet (508 m). To reflect Taiwan's culture, the building was designed to resemble sturdy bamboo stalks growing out of the ground. The 101-story building has 2.14 million square feet (198,348 sq m) of office space, and an additional 804,182 square feet (74,711 sq m) for a shopping center. As a safety precaution, the steel-frame building was built to withstand the country's strongest earthquakes and winds at a force of 134 miles (216 km) per hour.

City with the
Most Skyscrapers

Hong Kong

A total of 180 skyscrapers rise high above the streets of Hong Kong. In fact, the world's fifth-tallest building—Two International Finance Centre—towers 1,362 feet (415 m) above the city. Because this bustling Chinese business center only has about 160 square miles (414 sq km) of land that's suitable for building, architects have to build up instead of out. And Hong Kong just keeps growing—56 of the city's giants were built in the last five years. Some large development projects, such as the Sky Tower Apartment Complex, added seven skyscrapers to the landscape in just one year.

WORLD CITIES WITH
THE MOST SKYSCRAPERS

Number of skyscrapers

City	Number
Hong Kong, China	180
New York City, New York	178
Chicago, Illinois	82
Tokyo, Japan	55
Shanghai, China	50

World's Tallest
Apartment Building

Trump World Tower

Trump World Tower in New York City rises 863 feet (263 m) above Manhattan, making it the world's tallest apartment building. Located in the United Nations Plaza and built by billionaire Donald Trump, this 72-story engineering marvel offers truly luxurious condominiums. Some amenities include a private spa and health club, a world-class restaurant, a 60-foot (18.3-m) swimming pool, and a landscaped garden. Condos feature marble bathrooms, maple hardwood floors, 16-foot (4.8-m) ceilings, and state-of-the-art appliances. These spectacular homes range from $1.0 to $13.5 million.

THE WORLD'S TALLEST APARTMENT BUILDINGS

Height in feet/meters

863 ft. 263 m.	656 ft. 200 m.	645 ft. 197 m.	628 ft. 191 m.	599 ft. 183 m.
Trump World Towers, New York, USA	Tregunter Tower III, Hong Kong, China	Lake Point Tower, Chicago, USA	Central Park Place, New York, USA	Huron Plaza Apartments, Chicago, USA

World's Largest Mall

Golden Resources Shopping Mall

GOLDEN RESOURCES SHOPPING MALL

THE WORLD'S LARGEST MALLS

Area in millions of square feet/square meters

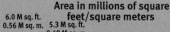

6.0 M sq. ft. 0.56 M sq. m.	5.3 M sq. ft. 0.49 M sq. m.	4.2 M sq. ft. 0.39 M sq. m.	3.0 M sq. ft. 0.28 M sq. m.	2.3 M sq. ft. 0.21 M sq. m.
Golden Resources Shopping Mall, China	West Edmonton Mall, Canada	Mall of America, Minnesota, USA	Del Amo Fashion Center, California, USA	Woodfield Shopping Center, Illinois, USA

The Golden Resources Shopping Mall in Beijing, China, offers consumers 6.0 million square feet (0.56 million sq m) of retail space under one roof. There are more than 1,000 shops to choose from, offering everything from Jaguar automobiles to generic shampoo. There is a food court that spans the length of two football fields. The giant glass-and-steel building opened in October 2004 and took just 20 months to complete. Although malls are becoming more popular in China, the success of Golden Resources is uncertain. The initial crowd of 50,000 shoppers a day has dropped off to just a few hundred.

263

Amusement Park with the
Most Rides

Cedar Point

Cedar Point in Sandusky, Ohio, has 68 rides for park goers to enjoy. Top Thrill Dragster—the park's newest roller coaster—is the tallest in the world at 420 feet (128 m). Another tall ride—the 300-foot (91-m) Power Tower—blasts riders up and down the towers at a speed of 55 miles (89 km) per hour. And with 16 roller coasters, Cedar Point also has the most coasters of any theme park in the world. More than 44,500 feet (13,564 m) of coaster track—more than 6 miles (9.7 km)—run through the park. Cedar Point opened in 1870 and is the second-oldest amusement park in the country.

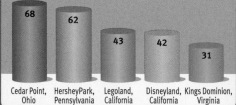

THE AMUSEMENT PARKS WITH THE MOST RIDES

Number of rides

Cedar Point, Ohio	HersheyPark, Pennsylvania	Legoland, California	Disneyland, California	Kings Dominion, Virginia
68	62	43	42	31

World's Highest City

Wenchuan, China

Wenchuan, China, sits 16,730 feet (5,103 m) above the sea. That's 3.2 miles (5.2 km) high, more than half the height of Mt. Everest. There are several ancient villages in the area with houses dating back hundreds of years. Located nearby is the Wolong Panda Preserve—one of the last places on Earth where the endangered bears are studied and bred. The city is part of the Sichuan Province, which is located in southwest China. The province covers 207,340 square miles (537,000 sq km) and has a population of 94.5 million.

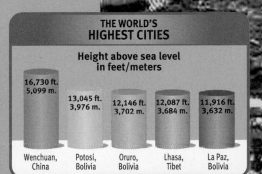

THE WORLD'S HIGHEST CITIES

Height above sea level in feet/meters

16,730 ft. 5,099 m.	13,045 ft. 3,976 m.	12,146 ft. 3,702 m.	12,087 ft. 3,684 m.	11,916 ft. 3,632 m.
Wenchuan, China	Potosi, Bolivia	Oruro, Bolivia	Lhasa, Tibet	La Paz, Bolivia

World's Most Massive Dam

Tarbela Dam

The Tarbela Dam on the Indus River in Pakistan can hold an amazing 5,244 million cubic feet (148.5 million cu m) of water. The dam measures 469 feet (143 m) high and 2,264 feet (691 m) thick at the base. The dam was built in 1976 by more than 15,000 workers and engineers at a cost of $900 million. Although the dam was originally built to store water for agricultural purposes, the release of water also produces electricity.

THE WORLD'S MOST MASSIVE DAMS

Volume in millions of cubic feet/meters

Dam	Volume
Tarbela, Pakistan	5,244 M cu. ft. 148.5 M cu. m.
Fort Peck, USA	3,390 M cu. ft. 96.0 M cu. m.
Tucurui, Brazil	3,009 M cu. ft. 85.2 M cu. m.
Ataturk, Turkey	3,002 M cu. ft. 85.0 M cu. m.
Yacireta, Argentina	2,861 cu. ft. 81.0 M cu. m.

World's Longest
Underwater Tunnel

Seikan Tunnel

The Seikan Tunnel stretches underwater for a total of 33.4 miles (53.8 km), making it both the longest railway tunnel and underwater tunnel in the world. It connects Honshu—the main island of Japan—to Hokkaido, an island to the north. Some 14.3 miles (23 km) of the tunnel run under the Tsugaru Strait, which connects the Pacific Ocean to the Sea of Japan. A railway in the tunnel transports passengers. Construction began in 1964 and took 24 years to complete. Today, the Seikan Tunnel is no longer the quickest way between the two islands. Air travel is faster and almost the same price.

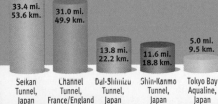

THE WORLD'S LONGEST UNDERWATER TUNNELS

Length in miles/kilometers

33.4 mi. 53.6 km.	31.0 mi. 49.9 km.	13.8 mi. 22.2 km.	11.6 mi. 18.8 km.	5.0 mi. 9.5 km.
Seikan Tunnel, Japan	Channel Tunnel, France/England	Dai-Shimizu Tunnel, Japan	Shin-Kanmo Tunnel, Japan	Tokyo Bay Aqualine, Japan

267

World's Longest Road Tunnel

Laerdal

The 15.2-mile (24.5-km) Laerdal Tunnel was officially opened in Norway on November 27, 2000. This huge construction makes its way under large mountain chains to connect the capital of Oslo to the port of Bergen, Norway's second-largest city. The tunnel is 29.5 feet (9 m) wide and 21 feet (6.3 m) high. It is estimated that about 1,000 cars and trucks make the 20-minute drive through the tunnel each day. To help make the tunnel safe, the designers installed fire extinguishers every 410 feet (125 m) and special lighting to keep drivers alert. There are also many parking spaces and turning areas in case drivers need to stop or have car trouble. The Laerdal Tunnel cost about $114 million to build.

THE WORLD'S LONGEST ROAD TUNNELS

Length in miles/kilometers

Laerdal, Norway	St. Gotthard, Switzerland	Arlberg, Austria	Frejus, France/Italy	Pinglin Highway, Taiwan
15.2 mi. 24.5 km.	10.3 mi. 16.4 km.	8.7 mi. 14.0 km.	8.0 mi. 12.9 km.	8.0 mi. 12.9 km.

Most-Visited National Park

Great Smoky Mountains

Each year, more than 9.36 million people travel to North Carolina and Tennessee to visit the Great Smoky Mountains. The national park is 521,225 acres (210,900 ha), about 95% of which is forested. While at the park, visitors can admire some of the area's many waterfalls while enjoying some 850 miles (1,368 km) of hiking trails and 550 miles (885 km) of horseback riding trails. Visitors may also see some of the park's 4,130 different plant and tree species or 300 bird and animal species.

GREAT SMOKY MOUNTAINS NATIONAL PARK

AN INTERNATIONAL BIOSPHERE RESERVE

THE UNITED STATES' MOST-VISITED NATIONAL PARKS

Annual visitors, in millions

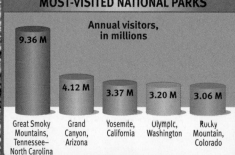

Park	Annual visitors (millions)
Great Smoky Mountains, Tennessee–North Carolina	9.36 M
Grand Canyon, Arizona	4.12 M
Yosemite, California	3.37 M
Olympic, Washington	3.20 M
Rocky Mountain, Colorado	3.06 M

World's
Busiest Airport

Hartsfield Atlanta International Airport

In one year, an average of more than 79 million passengers travel through the Hartsfield Atlanta International Airport. That's more people than are living in California, Texas, and Florida combined. Approximately 2,200 planes depart and arrive at this airport every day. With parking lots, runways, maintenance facilities, and other buildings, the Hartsfield terminal complex covers about 130 acres (53 ha). Hartsfield Atlanta International Airport has a north and a south terminal, as well as an underground train and six concourses that feature many shops, restaurants, and banks.

THE WORLD'S BUSIEST AIRPORTS

Annual passengers, in millions

Hartsfield Atlanta Intl., USA	Chicago O'Hare Intl., USA	Heathrow Intl., England	Haneda Intl., Japan	Los Angeles Intl., USA
79.1 M	69.5 M	63.5 M	62.9 M	54.9 M

Country with the
Most Airports

The United States

The United States leads the world with 14,807 airports. That is more than the number of airports for the other nine top countries combined. The top two busiest airports in the world are also located in the United States. All together, U.S. airports serve more than 697 million travelers a year. With the threat of terrorism and the state of the economy, the airline industry lost $10 billion in 2002. But during the past few years, airline travel has picked up due to discount airlines and competitive ticket pricing.

THE COUNTRIES WITH THE MOST AIRPORTS

Number of airports

USA	Brazil	Russia	Mexico	Argentina
14,807	3,803	2,609	1,827	1,335

World's Top
Tourist Country

France

Each year, about 75 million tourists visit France. That's more than twice the number of people living in all of New England combined. The most popular French destinations are Paris and the Mediterranean coast. In July and August—the most popular months to visit France—tourists flock to the westernmost coastal areas of the region. In the winter, visitors hit the slopes at major ski resorts in the northern Alps. Tourists also visit many of France's world-renowned landmarks and monuments, including the Eiffel Tower, Notre Dame, the Louvre, and the Arc de Triomphe. Most tourists are from other European countries, especially Germany.

THE WORLD'S TOP
TOURIST COUNTRIES

International visitors, in millions

France	Spain	USA	Italy	China
75.0 M	52.5 M	40.4 M	39.6 M	33.0 M

World's Most-Visited City

New York City

THE WORLD'S MOST-VISITED CITIES

Annual visitors, in millions

City	Visitors
New York City, USA	39.6 M
Tijuana, Mexico	35.0 M
Paris, France	25.0 M
Hong Kong, China	21.8 M
London, England	19.0 M

More than 39 million tourists visited New York City in just one year. That's the equivalent of the entire population of Canada coming for vacation! Both domestic and international travelers come to New York City to enjoy the theater and performing arts, museums, shopping, and historical landmarks. Collectively, visitors contribute more than $15 billion to the city's economy annually. Just more than 5 million tourists are from other countries, and most come from the United Kingdom, Canada, and Japan. During their stay, most travelers take advantage of the city's 70,545 hotel rooms and 17,312 restaurants.

273

Country with the Most Bicycles per Capita

The Netherlands

With an estimated 17.6 million bicycles in the country, the Netherlands has more bicycles per capita than any other nation. It averages to more than one bike for every person in the country. Many people around the world—especially those in crowded cities—have realized that bicycling is an easy way to get around and a great way to cut down on pollution. The Netherlands, in particular, is battling a major pollution problem, and it is one of the world's most densely populated nations.

COUNTRIES WITH THE MOST BICYCLES PER CAPITA

Bikes per person

Netherlands	Germany	Japan	USA	China
1.10	0.88	0.63	0.49	0.37

Country with the
Most Cars

The United States

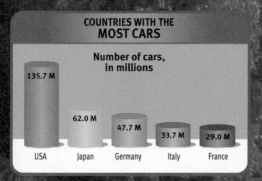

COUNTRIES WITH THE MOST CARS

Number of cars, in millions

135.7 M — USA
62.0 M — Japan
47.7 M — Germany
33.7 M — Italy
29.0 M — France

The citizens of the United States own 135.7 million automobiles. That's about 30% of all the automobiles owned in the world. It means that for every two Americans there is one car. That figure doesn't even include all of the trucks, campers, and motorcycles in the country. Almost 90% of all U.S. residents have access to motor vehicles. With 18.7 million cars, California is the state with the most registered automobiles in the nation. Each year, U.S. drivers total about 4.2 trillion passenger miles (6.8 million passenger km) of travel and burn about 200 billion gallons (757 billion l) of fuel. The average American driver also spends about 22 hours each year stuck in traffic.

Country with the Most Roads

The United States

THE COUNTRIES WITH THE MOST ROADS

Miles/kilometers of roads

- USA — 3,980,688 mi. 6,406,296 km.
- India — 2,083,358 mi. 3,352,840 km.
- Brazil — 1,080,401 mi. 1,738,737 km.
- China — 878,368 mi. 1,413,596 km.
- Japan — 727,577 mi. 1,170,922 km.

There are 3,980,688 miles (6,406,296 km) of roads that crisscross the United States. Approximately 2.6 million miles (4.2 million km) of these roads are paved. About three-quarters of the roads, or 2.9 million miles (4.7 million km), are part of the national road system. Each person in America makes an average of four outings and travels some 44 miles (71 km) each day. Because Americans are always on the move, it's not surprising that the nation's highways are frequently tied up with traffic jams. Americans waste about 7 billion gallons (26.5 billion l) of fuel and 4.3 billion hours annually because they are stuck in traffic.

City with the Busiest
Subway System

Moscow

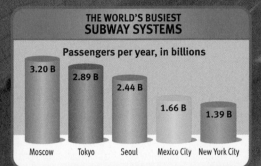

THE WORLD'S BUSIEST SUBWAY SYSTEMS

Passengers per year, in billions

Moscow	Tokyo	Seoul	Mexico City	New York City
3.20 B	2.89 B	2.44 B	1.66 B	1.39 B

Each year, more than 3 billion people ride on Moscow's bustling Metropolitan (Metro) subway system. It is not only busy, it is also world renowned for its beautiful architecture. Many of the 150 stations have stained glass, marble statuary, and sparkling chandeliers. The rail network is 153 miles (246 km) long and follows the street pattern above. About half of the subway riders travel for free because they are students, retirees, police officers, or military personnel. Other riders pay 7 rubles, or about 25 cents, per ride.

Money and
Business Records

Most Valuable • Industry • Wealth

World's Most Valuable
Pop Memorabilia

John Lennon's Phantom V Rolls-Royce

Jim Pattison with John Lennon's Phantom V Rolls-Royce

THE WORLD'S MOST
VALUABLE POP MEMORABILIA

Cost at auction

$2.29 M	$2.15 M	$850,000	$491,500	$455,500
John Lennon's Phantom V Rolls-Royce	John Lennon's Steinway Model Z Piano	Jerry Garcia's Guitar "Tiger"	Eric Clapton's Guitar "Brownie"	John Lennon's "Nowhere Man" Lyrics

At a Sotheby's auction in 1983, Jim Pattison's company—Ripley International Inc.—bought John Lennon's Phantom V Rolls-Royce touring limousine for $2.29 million. Lennon, of the group The Beatles, bought the car in 1965. Quickly bored with the plain black exterior, Lennon had the car painted in psychedelic colors and designs. In 1970, Lennon had the Phantom V shipped to the United States and loaned it to several rock stars, including the Rolling Stones, the Moody Blues, and Bob Dylan.

279

World's Most Valuable Comic Book

Action Comics Number 1

Action Comics Number 1 is the most valuable comic book in the world with an auction price of $350,000. It was published in June 1938 and was the first comic book to feature Superman. Action Comics printed about 700 issues in the series. Traditionally, the first comic book of any series is the most valuable. Although thousands of copies of this issue were produced and circulated, only about 75 remain. And only four of these copies are in mint condition. Paper drives during World War II destroyed many early comic books.

THE WORLD'S MOST VALUABLE COMIC BOOKS

By auction price

Action Comics No. 1	Detective Comics No. 27	Marvel Comics No. 1	Superman No. 1	All American Comics No. 16
$350,000	$300,000	$250,000	$210,000	$115,000

World's Most Valuable
Production Car

Saleen S7

THE WORLD'S MOST VALUABLE PRODUCTION CARS*

Base price

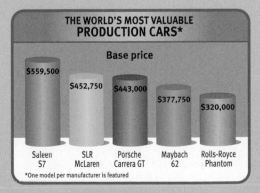

Saleen S7	SLR McLaren	Porsche Carrera GT	Maybach 62	Rolls-Royce Phantom
$559,500	$452,750	$443,000	$377,750	$320,000

*One model per manufacturer is featured

The base price for a Saleen S7 is a cool $559,500. That's about 3 times more than the price of the average home in the United States! And, the car actually costs $120,000 more than it did last year, mostly due to engine improvements. The Saleen S7 has a V-8 engine with 750 horsepower—the highest horsepower of any car in the United States. It can accelerate from 0 to 60 in under three seconds, and can reach a top speed of more than 200 miles (322 km) per hour. Each car is custom-built for its owner.

Most Expensive
Movie Memorabilia

Best Film Oscar®
for *Gone With
the Wind*

*David Selznick receiving the
Oscar®* for Gone With the Wind.

David Selznick's Best Film Oscar® for
producing the film classic *Gone With the
Wind* was purchased by pop superstar
Michael Jackson for $1.54 million.
Jackson's agent called Sotheby's in June
1999 and entered into a bidding war for
the coveted award. Eventually, the
Oscar® went to Jackson for a price that
was more than five times higher than its
estimated value of $300,000. Jackson
said it was his lifelong dream to own the
Oscar®. Memorabilia from *Gone With the
Wind*—the 1939 film starring Vivien Leigh
and Clark Gable—has long been
especially popular and often fetches
a high price on the auction block.

282

**THE WORLD'S MOST EXPENSIVE
MOVIE MEMORABILIA SOLD AT AUCTION**

Price paid in US dollars

$1,540,000	$666,000	$578,000	$562,500	$507,500
David Selznick's *Gone With the Wind* Oscar®	Judy Garland's Ruby Slippers	Bette Davis's *Jezebel* Oscar®	Vivien Leigh's *Gone With the Wind* Oscar®	Clark Gable's *It Happened One Night* Oscar®

World's Most Valuable Television

Runco MBX-1

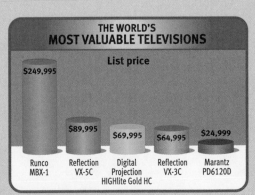

THE WORLD'S MOST VALUABLE TELEVISIONS

List price

$249,995				
	$89,995	$69,995	$64,995	$24,999
Runco MBX-1	Reflection VX-5C	Digital Projection HIGHlite Gold HC	Reflection VX-3C	Marantz PD6120D

With a $249,995 price tag, the Runco MBX-1 is the most valuable television in the world. Although it is classified as a TV, this pricey home entertainment unit works just like a projector. The television programming enters the projector like it would in a normal television set, and then the unit projects the images onto a screen or wall. This digital projector can fill a screen up to 500 inches (12.7 m) wide—about the width of an average movie screen—with perfect clarity.

World's Most Valuable
Baseball

Mark McGwire's 70th Home Run Baseball

Businessman and baseball fan Todd McFarlane made sports history himself when he paid $3.05 million for Mark McGwire's 70th home run baseball in January 1999. The bid, which was actually $2.7 million plus a large commission fee, is the most money paid for a sports artifact. The ball was only expected to sell for about $1 million. McFarlane said he bought the ball because he wanted to own a piece of history. This famous baseball marked the end of the exciting 1998 home run race between Mark McGwire and Sammy Sosa. Both beat Roger Maris's three-decade record of 61—Sosa with 66 and McGwire with 70.

THE WORLD'S MOST VALUABLE BASEBALLS

Price paid at auction, in US dollars

$3.05 M	$517,500	$150,000	$125,500	$106,600
McGwire's 70th Home Run Baseball	Bonds' 73rd Home Run Baseball	Sosa's 66th Home Run Baseball	Ruth's First Yankee Stadium Home Run Baseball	Cubs' 2003 Playoffs Foul Ball

World's Most Profitable
Food Brand

Coca-Cola

Coca-Cola is the most profitable food brand in the world, earning $21.9 billion in revenue in 2004. Coca-Cola was invented in the United States by John Pemberton in 1887. He quickly trademarked his mix of Coca-Cola syrup and carbonated water and it became a popular fountain drink. Today about 300 different Coca-Cola products can be found in 200 countries around the globe. Most well-known brands like Coke and Sprite are widely available, but some countries have their own special flavors. For instance, Brazilians enjoy Bonaqua, the Japanese drink Sokebicha, and Israelis may quench their thirst with Kinley.

THE WORLD'S MOST
PROFITABLE FOOD BRANDS

Sales in billions of US dollars

Coca-Cola	McDonald's	Budweiser	Nescafé	Pepsi
$21.9 B	$19.0 B	$14.9 B	$12.0 B	$10.9 B

Country That Spends the Most on Toys

United States

**COUNTRIES THAT
SPEND THE MOST ON TOYS**

Annual per capita spending

USA	UK	France	Japan	Germany
$121	$113	$71	$70	$63

In 2004, Americans spent an amazing $35.1 billion on toys! That's equivalent to every single person in the country buying $121 worth of toys! It's not too much of a surprise considering toys are sold practically everywhere from grocery stores to hardware stores. Wal-Mart averages the highest toy sales with 22% of the market, followed by Toys "R" Us with 14%. The United States also leads the world in toy development, marketing, and advertising and employs more than 32,000 people in those fields.

World's Largest International Food Franchise

McDonald's

THE WORLD'S LARGEST INTERNATIONAL FOOD FRANCHISES

Number of franchises

McDonald's	Subway	KFC	Burger King	Pizza Hut
30,221	22,481	13,015	11,648	10,831

There are more than 30,000 McDonald's restaurants in the world, serving customers in 119 different countries. McDonald's serves about 50 million customers each day, about 24 million of whom are in the United States. Some of the most popular McDonald's menu items include the Big Mac, the Quarter Pounder, the Egg McMuffin, and Chicken McNuggets. Out of respect for local cultures, restaurants in different countries modify their menus according to religious or cultural traditions. For example, there is a kosher McDonald's in Jerusalem, and the Big Macs in India are made with lamb instead of beef.

U.S. Company with the
Highest-Paid CEO

Colgate-Palmolive

U.S. COMPANIES WITH THE HIGHEST-PAID CEOs

2004 earnings in millions of US dollars

Company	Earnings
Colgate-Palmolive	$147.9 M
United Technologies	$70.5 M
Lehman Brothers Holding	$67.7 M
Cendant	$60.0 M
NVR	$58.1 M

Mark Reuben earns a whopping $147,970,000 a year for his job as chief executive officer at Colgate-Palmolive. That's 370 times the salary of the president of the United States. Reuben has been with the company for more than 40 years, and has served as CEO since 1984. The Harvard grad is credited with helping the company update its product line and reinvent itself by incorporating creative marketing strategies. Colgate-Palmolive is best known for producing toothpaste, deodorant, household cleaners, and pet food.

World's Top-Selling Car

Toyota Camry

THE WORLD'S TOP-SELLING CARS

Total sold in 2004

426,990	386,770	333,161	309,196	248,148
Toyota Camry	Honda Accord	Toyota Corolla	Honda Civic	Ford Taurus

The Toyota Camry was the most popular car in 2004, with sales totaling 426,990 vehicles. The Camry has a standard 2.4 litre, 16 valve engine and features cruise control, keyless entry, and a state-of-the-art audio system. The Camry has also been rated as one of the safest cars on the road. In addition to front, overhead, and side-impact airbags, the car features Vehicle Skid Control brakes.

World's Richest Country

Luxembourg

Luxembourg is a very small country in western Europe. It has a gross domestic product of $55,100 per person. The gross domestic product is calculated by dividing the annual worth of all the goods and services produced in a country by the country's population. Luxembourg's low inflation and low unemployment help to keep the economy solid. The industrial sector makes up a large part of the country's gross domestic product and includes products such as iron and steel, food processing, chemicals, metal products, engineering, tires, glass, and aluminum. The country's financial sector also plays a significant role in the economy, accounting for about 22% of the gross domestic product.

THE WORLD'S RICHEST COUNTRIES

Gross domestic product per capita in US dollars

Luxembourg	Norway	USA	Switzerland	Denmark
$55,100	$37,800	$37,800	$32,700	$31,100

World's
Poorest Country

Sierra Leone

Sierra Leone, a small country on Africa's northwest coast, has a gross domestic product of just $500. Although the country does have solid agricultural, mineral, and fishing resources, the government has not been able to take full advantage of them because of frequent war and social uprising. In the near future, the country hopes to reopen the many mines closed down because of the fighting. Sierra Leone has managed to maintain its diamond mining throughout the wars. The majority of the country makes a living from agriculture and manufacturing. Sierra Leone also receives a large amount of aid from abroad.

THE WORLD'S
POOREST COUNTRIES

Gross domestic product per capita in US dollars

Sierra Leone	East Timor	Somalia	Burundi	Tanzania
$500	$550	$550	$600	$600

World's Richest Man

Bill Gates

Bill Gates is probably one of the world's most recognizable businesspeople. He is the co-founder of Microsoft— the most valuable computer software company in the world—and he is worth an incredible $46.5 billion. As Microsoft's largest individual shareholder, Gates became a billionaire on paper when the company went public in 1986. Since then, Gates has been very generous with his fortune. Through his Gates Foundation, he has donated billions of dollars to health research, libraries, and education.

THE WORLD'S RICHEST MEN

Assets in billions of US dollars

Bill Gates, USA	Warren Buffett, USA	Lakshmi Mittal, India	Carlos Slim Helú, Mexico	Prince Alwaleed Bin Talal Alsaud, Saudi Arabia
$46.5 B	$44.0 B	$25.0 B	$23.8 B	$23.7 B

World's Richest Women

Alice and Helen Walton

With an estimated worth of $18 billion each, Helen Walton and her daughter Alice are the richest women in the world. They are two of the heirs to the Walton family fortune, amassed by Helen's husband, entrepreneur Sam Walton. He opened the first Wal-Mart store in 1962 and turned it into one of the most successful businesses in American history. Today, Wal-Mart is the world's largest retailer. The Walton Family Foundation was set up as a way for the Waltons to give back to their country. Schools, church groups, community projects, hospitals, and many other organizations throughout the United States receive donations.

THE WORLD'S RICHEST WOMEN

Assets in billions of US dollars

$18.0 B	$18.0 B	$17.2 B	$12.0 B	$11.7 B	$11.7 B
Alice L. Walton, USA	Helen R. Walton, USA	Lilianne Bettencourt, France	Abigail Johnson, USA	Barbara Cox Anthony, USA	Anne Cox Chambers, USA

Helen Walton

293

World's Youngest Billionaire

Athina Onassis Roussel

Greek shipping tycoon Aristotle Onassis left his granddaughter well provided for. When Athina Onassis Roussel turned 18 years old in 2003, she inherited an estimated $2.7 billion in properties, including an island in the Ionian Sea, companies, shares, artwork, and a private jet. At 21, she became president of the Athens-based Onassis Foundation and received another $2 billion. She became the only heir to the Onassis shipping fortune when her mother, Christina, died in 1988. Currently, the estate is being managed by financial advisers. Athina lives in a small village near Lausanne, Switzerland, with her father, Thierry Roussel, and her stepfamily. She speaks fluent English, French, and Swedish, and enjoys playing sports and horseback riding.

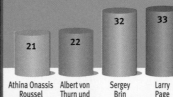

THE WORLD'S YOUNGEST BILLIONAIRES

Age in 2006

Athina Onassis Roussel	Albert von Thurn und Taxis	Sergey Brin	Larry Page	Andrei Melnichenko
21	22	32	33	34

World's All-Time
Richest Person

John D. Rockefeller's 1913 fortune of $900 million would be worth about $189 billion in current U.S. dollars. Rockefeller made his money from the Standard Oil Company, which he co-founded in 1870. By 1911, he controlled most of the oil production and transportation industries in the United States. Rockefeller was one of the nation's leading philanthropists and was quite generous with his money. In fact, he donated more than $500 million during his lifetime. His son, John Rockefeller, Jr., donated about $2.5 billion of the family fortune to charitable causes.

THE WORLD'S RICHEST PEOPLE OF ALL TIME

Estimated wealth in current billions of US dollars

$189.0 B	$100.0 B	$96.0 B	$46.5 B	$44.0 B
John D. Rockefeller, USA	Andrew Carnegie, USA	Cornelius Vanderbilt, USA	Bill Gates, USA	Warren Buffet, USA

John D. Rockefeller

Index

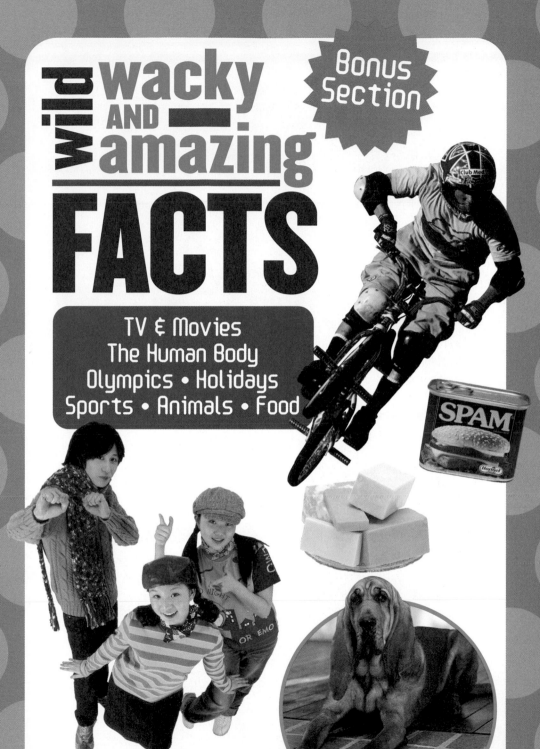

wild wacky AND amazing FACTS

Bonus Section

TV & Movies
The Human Body
Olympics • Holidays
Sports • Animals • Food

This Guy Is Golden

Jamie Foxx is the first person to have been nominated for three top acting awards at the Golden Globes in the same year. The 2005 nominations were for Best Performance By An Actor In A Motion Picture—Musical Or Comedy (*Ray*), Best Performance By An Actor In A Supporting Role In A Motion Picture (*Collateral*), and Best Performance By An Actor In A Mini-Series Or A Motion Picture Made For Television (*Redemption*). Foxx won the Best Actor award for his portrayal of music legend Ray Charles in *Ray*.

No Kidding!

Movie star Nicole Kidman became the highest-paid commercial actress when she starred in a three-minute advertisement for Chanel No.5 and earned $3.1 million. That equals about $17,222 per second. In the ad, Kidman plays a movie star running away from photographers. She also got to wear more than $40 million in diamonds during the filming.

Not Just Another Pretty Face

Although Ashton Kutcher plays some pretty ditzy characters on TV and in the movies, he actually studied biochemical engineering at the University of Iowa. While in school, he earned extra cash by sweeping up Cheerios dust at the General Mills plant and donating blood. One night he entered a modeling contest for fun and got a runway job in New York just two days later. He left the Cheerios sweeping behind but says he still likes to eat them.

World Series Rework

Fever Pitch tells the story of a man's love of the Boston Red Sox. Many of the baseball scenes were filmed when the team was in the 2004 playoffs. When the Red Sox made it to the World Series just before the movie was set to wrap, the film's ending had to quickly be rewritten to include the team's successful postseason. The scene in which Drew Barrymore and Jimmy Fallon celebrate on the field was shot during the actual game-ending inning of the World Series. Fans watching the live TV broadcast got a glimpse of the movie when the film crew was accidentally picked up on the air.

A Wizard's Wealth

Daniel Radcliffe has earned more than $11.5 million portraying Harry Potter. This makes him the wealthiest teenager in Britain. Although he got paid about $110,000 for the first film, he now earns about $3 million per picture.

Here Today, Gone Tomorrow

In a lifetime, a person will shed more than 40 pounds (18 kg) of skin. Every minute, some 35,000 dead skin cells fall from the body. Most of these cells collect with dust and are later eaten by dust mites.

Tongue Twister

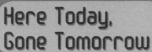

Similar to fingerprints, everyone in the world has a different tongue print. About 9,000 taste buds cover the tongue and are replaced about every two weeks. As people age, some of the taste buds do not get replaced. As a result of the continuously changing surface, no two tongues are identical.

Winkin', Blinkin', and Nod

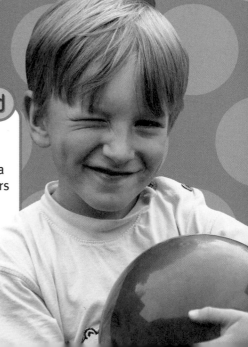

The human eye blinks an average of 15,000 times a day. This means that a person blinks about 5.5 million times a year—the equivalent of about 152 hours of automatic shut-eye. When the eye is open, it can process 36,000 bits of information every hour. In an average life span, a person will see almost 24 million images.

No Bones About It

The adult skeleton contains 206 bones, but the skeleton of a baby contains 350. As the baby grows, some of the bones fuse together. A person's bones are not evenly distributed throughout the body—more than half are found in the hands and feet.

A Nose Knows

Most people can distinguish between 3,000 to 10,000 different smells. However, about 2 million people in the United States can smell nothing at all. This disorder is called anosmia and is usually caused when the olfactory bulb in the nose has been injured.

Speedy Signals

The body's nervous system can transmit messages to the brain at an amazing 180 miles (290 km) per hour—three times faster than the speed limit on most highways. Each nerve can transmit about 1,000 impulses each second!

NEVE   GLIZ

Mascots That Melt

The 2006 Winter Olympics in Torino, Italy, will have two official greeters. Neve is a graceful snowball and Gliz is a playful ice cube. Together they physically represent the elements needed for the games—snow and ice.

Who Needs Wings?

When a skier launches off an Olympic ski jump, he or she will travel approximately 395 feet (120 m) in the air. That's the same length as 10 school buses lined end to end. The jumper usually remains in the air for less than 10 seconds, meaning that he or she is traveling almost 27 miles (43.5 km) per hour.

Super-Speedy Sled

Olympic skeleton racers fly down the icy course at a top speed of 85 miles (137 km) per hour. The sleds have no brakes and no steering wheels. The only way for the athletes to stop is by running out of speed or running into something.

In Need of a Medal Detector

Although most people would remember winning an Olympic medal for the rest of their lives, a few winners from the Athens games apparently forgot to bring theirs home. Chilean tennis player Nicolas Massu left his medal in the cab going to the airport. And Dutch rower Diederik Simon left his medal on his bed in Olympic Village. Luckily, both medals were returned to the owners.

Wintertime Wins

Only two countries south of the equator have won medals in the Olympic Games—New Zealand and Australia. New Zealand's first cold-weather medal came in 1992 when skier Annelise Coberger won silver in the slalom in Albertville, France. Australia's first medal in the Winter Olympic Games came in 1998 when Zali Steggall finished third in the Alpine skiing slalom event, in Nagano, Japan. At the 2002 Olympics in Salt Lake City, Utah, Australia picked up two more medals. Alisa Camplin won gold in the women's freestyle skiing aerials, and Steven Bradbury took gold in the men's 1000 meter speed skate.

International Dog Biscuit Appreciation Day

(February 23) Dogs around the world will be celebrating. The crispy canine cookies were the first commercially prepared pet food. They were originally sold in England in the 1860s.

(May 14) Hit the floor with friends and get funky. The melody for the "Chicken Dance" was written in the late 1950s by Swiss accordion player Werner Thomas. When the song was played in the United States in the early 1980s, audiences made up a dance to go along with it. Today the "Chicken Dance" is played at millions of parties and weddings across the country.

Dance Like a Chicken Day

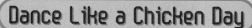

Wiggle Your Toes Day

(August 6) Set those piggies free today! Of the 26 bones in your foot, 19 are toe bones called phalanges.

International Talk Like a Pirate Day

(September 19) Yo-ho-ho and shiver me timbers! Don't let any scalawags hornswoggle you out of celebrating like a buccaneer today.

Moldy Cheese Day

(October 9) Hold your nose and rejoice in these delicious dairy products. Some cheeses—such as Roquefort, blue, and gorgonzola—are actually made by introducing mold into them.

Look on the Bright Side Day

(December 21) Take a cheery outlook on things today—it could improve your health. Optimists are 25% less likely to get sick than pessimists.

A Hush Falls over the Crowd

There are only two days in the entire year when no professional sports games—including the NBA, MLB, NHL, and NFL—are held. They are the day before and the day after the MLB All-Star Game.

Seeing Stars

Pro basketball player Yao Ming received 2,558,278 votes for the All-Star team in 2005—more than any other player in NBA history. The 7.5-foot (2.3-m) Ming plays for the Houston Rockets during the regular season.

Mirra Mania

Freestyle BMX legend Dave Mirra has won 18 medals at the X Games—more than any other competitor. Mirra has been a pro for fourteen years and was the first rider to land a double backflip in competition. All of his crazy stunts have earned him the nickname "Miracle Boy." He even has his own video game on Playstation 2.

He's Definitely Got Game

Defensive tackle Mike Lodish has played in 6 Super Bowls, more than any other player. He competed in four straight NFL championships with the Buffalo Bills from 1991 to 1994, but failed to earn a Super Bowl ring. Then he returned in 1998 and 1999 with the Denver Broncos and celebrated victory both times.

Most people would think sports stars eat super-nutritious foods before competition, but some have other favorites. New York Yankees slugger Alex Rodriguez likes to start his day with a bowl full of Cocoa Puffs. Skateboarder Tony Hawk grabs some Bagel Bites before he jumps on his board. Eagles quarterback Donovan McNabb chows down on pancakes and sausages when he wakes up. And race car driver Jeff Gordon can't get enough ice cream.

The Breakfast of Champions?

Super Sniffers

The bloodhound's sense of smell is very reliable. It's more than 1,000 times more powerful than a human's. The dogs' sense of smell is most powerful in the winter, or in cold climates. When a dog is hot, its constant panting dries out its nose cells, which makes them less receptive to scents.

Got Milk?

A cow gives about 29,000 gallons (109,777 l) of milk in her lifetime. At that rate, it would take a small herd of about 27 cows almost 10 years to fill an Olympic-sized swimming pool.

Wicked Water Wasps

The deadliest sea creature in the world is the sea wasp. This jellyfish has a basketball-sized body with up to 60 tentacles measuring about 15 feet (4.6 m) long. The venom from just one creature can kill up to 60 adults. And if you get stung, death can happen in just 4 minutes. Sea wasps are found off the north coast of Australia and in the waters off southeast Asia.

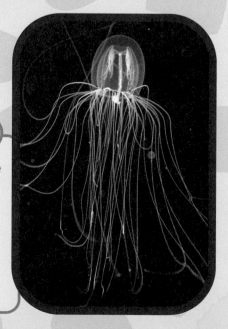

No Bones About It

A crocodile's digestive juices are so strong that it can digest a steel nail. Although the animals don't eat many nails, they do consume almost all of their prey—including horns, hooves, and bones. Their super-acidic stomach juices eat right through these solid snacks and allow them to exit the stomach.

Flying High

The Ruppell's Vulture can fly along at altitudes of more than 36,900 feet (937 m). This is 6,000 feet (152 m) higher than the cruising altitude of a commercial jet. Vultures have the slowest wing beat of any bird at 1 beat per second. They can fly at about 40 miles (64 km) per hour.

Violet Veggies, Anyone?

About 400 years ago, carrots were available in purple, red, yellow, and black. During the 17th century, the Dutch produced the orange carrot because it was the same color as their flag, and that variety became the favorite. Today farmers are putting colors back in carrots. The super-nutritious purple veggies are already on sale in Britain, and U.S. growers hope to introduce them soon. But they won't be entirely different—although the outside color is new, the centers will still be bright orange.

Pizza by the Pound

Americans pack away more than 1.3 billion pizzas each year. That's enough pie to cover 32,850 acres (13,294 ha) of land! The annual per capita consumption rate is 23 pounds (10 kg). The most popular topping is pepperoni, while the least favorite is anchovies. The most pizza is consumed on Saturday.

SPAM-alicious

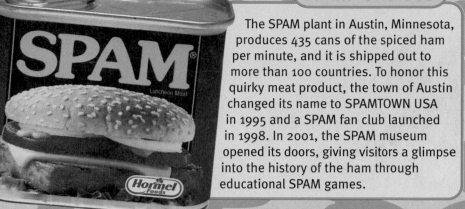

The SPAM plant in Austin, Minnesota, produces 435 cans of the spiced ham per minute, and it is shipped out to more than 100 countries. To honor this quirky meat product, the town of Austin changed its name to SPAMTOWN USA in 1995 and a SPAM fan club launched in 1998. In 2001, the SPAM museum opened its doors, giving visitors a glimpse into the history of the ham through educational SPAM games.

Fun with Flavors

Although vanilla and chocolate are always popular, some ice-cream makers are catering to unusual tastes. Some of the more unique flavors that made it to ice-cream parlors include mashed potato and bacon, tuna fish, fried pork rind, chili con carne, garlic, sauerkraut, mustard, dill pickle, and ketchup.

Cricket Cuisine

Entomophagy—the practice of eating insects—is common throughout the world. In fact, more than 1,000 insect species can be consumed in various ways. In the United States, ants, crickets, grasshoppers, and mealworms are the most common insects used for cooking. They can be roasted, fried, or dipped in chocolate. Many bookstores now carry recipe books so cooks can enjoy these crunchy critters at home.

On-the-go reference books for your on-the-go life!

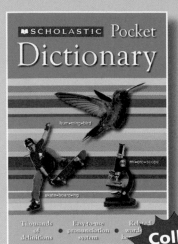
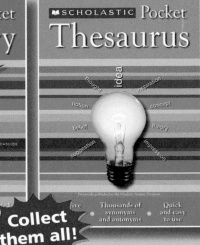
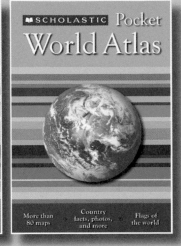